THR   A

QUIZ

SANAT PAI RAIKAR

BlueRose
Publishers
New Delhi • London

First Published in November 2021

ISBN: 978-93-5472-525-8

BLUEROSE PUBLISHERS

www.bluerosepublishers.com
info@bluerosepublishers.com
+91 8882 898 898

Cover Design:
Shreya

Typographic Design:
Namrata Saini

Distributed by: BlueRose, Amazon, Flipkart, Shopclues

DEDICATION

To A and B, for instilling a lifelong love for learning

To JS Sir, who let me 'borrow' quiz books and taught me so much without ever teaching me in a class

And most of all to N, for picking quizzes over movies on Friday nights

CONTENTS

ACKNOWLEDGEMENTS

Writing a book is no easy feat, much less attempting to write one from memory with minimal references. Compiling over twenty years of knowledge gained from participating in and conducting quizzes into book form has been an intense, but in the end, a rewarding process. For this, there are many people to thank.

Firstly, my lovely wife and daughter, who have put up with me locking myself up in a room on weekends to work on the book. We've had precious little time to spend together in the lockdown year, and I humbly thank you for letting me take some of that to myself to write this book.

I would also like to thank our extended families for their support and constant encouragement while working on this book. I am guilty of spending less time with all of you, and I hope to make up for this soon.

I want to thank my fellow quizzers and quizzing groups for their feedback, motivation and validation of the question samples I kept throwing their way. My quiz groups are a key portion of my life and I owe thanks to all of you.

And lastly, I want to thank you, the reader and my fellow quizzer, for picking up this book and reading it.

THE STORY BEHIND THIS BOOK

In the relatively mild summer of 2018, N and I were indulging in our usual Friday pastime of posing each other quiz questions. After the fifth instance of my making a statement that sounded something like, "Hey! I know this answer. I asked this question back in 2004 in so-and-so quiz," N, totally vexed, retorted, "If you remember so many of your questions, why don't you write a quiz book from memory?"

In a sudden rush of enthusiasm more associated with my (relatively) younger days, I accepted the challenge. The next step was to find some time out of a hectic work schedule to work on the book. I took a week off work, locked myself up in a room with no gadgets (and thus no temptation to 'Google' for questions) and went about creating chapters, and following a MECE (a fallout of my consulting career) approach to making up answers. Four days later, I emerged with a stubble and 650+ answers structured into 16 chapters.

The next step involved framing the questions to these answers. Progress was made on weekends, slow and steady, until the lockdown hit and all semblance of personal time went for a toss. But like the proverbial tortoise, the last twelve months saw gradual increments to these pages. All questions were written from memory (with some fact-checking to ensure I don't commit the worst crime a quizmaster can – that of incorrect facts). That said, any errors that may have crept in are solely my own and I will be happy to correct them if brought to my attention.

It has been a journey of over two years but a very enriching one. As most of these questions come from memory, this is as much a collection of quiz questions as a peek into my quizzing journey. I hope you derive as much pleasure from being posed the questions in these pages, as I did in setting them there.

1. LOVE, SEX, DHOKHA

"Sex sells", the classic marketing mantra goes, so it made sense to start off with a scandalous topic. Of course, betrayals don't always go hand in hand with love and sex, but the combination has been made very popular by the Dibakar Banerjee classic. So here goes.

Set 1

1. What work, believed to have been written between 1591 and 1595, features supporting characters such as Mercutio and Count Paris?

2. Which 1989 Palme d'Or winning film helped launch its director Steven Soderbergh to fame?

3. Which person, who headed a collaborationist regime by siding with the occupying forces, became synonymous with the word 'traitor'?

4. Which plant, with a hallucinogenic and narcotic root, was in ancient times used variously as an anaesthetic, hypnotic and most famously as an aphrodisiac? Some tales speak of the root screaming as it was pulled from the ground, killing anyone who heard it.

5. In the early 2000s, research (later questioned) claimed that 8% of the men in a region of Asia (16 million at the time of publication of the article) contained a Y-chromosomal lineage of

which famous conqueror, who was also renowned for his prowess in another field?

6. Which banking family, who was conferred a title meaning "merchant of the world", played a key role in the imprisonment and ultimate killing of Nawab Siraj-ud-Daulah of Bengal?

7. In early 1967, the BBC approached this iconic group to participate in what was to be the first ever live global television link (to 26 countries). They were asked to create something that would be understood by viewers of all nationalities. What resulted?

8. Which god, with the upper body of a man and the hind quarters, legs and horns of a goat, was recognized as the god of fields, groves and woods? He was also affiliated with sex and thus connected to fertility.

9. In Frank Miller's comic miniseries 300, who betrays the Spartans to Xerxes, showing the latter a trail allowing his forces to bypass the Spartans gathered at Thermopylae?

10. The daughter of Ashwapati and sister of Yudhajit, who plays a central role in the Ayodhya Kanda of the Ramayana?

11. Which goddess in Hindu mythology derives her name from the Sanskrit for 'enjoy' or 'delight in', and is believed to have been born from the sweat of Prajapati Daksha?

12. This film is based on a 1926 novella called 'Traumnovelle'. The director acquired rights to

the film in the 1960s but got to making the movie only 30 years later. It ended up being the last film he directed. Which erotic thriller am I talking about?

13. Who is known for something he did everyday at the Shibuya station in Tokyo for nine years, nine months, fifteen days, ending only with his death on March 8, 1935?

14. How is Rohypnol, known to cause anterograde amnesia, more commonly known as, largely due to its role in drug-facilitated sexual assaults?

Set 2

1. Which king rejected Papal authority and initiated the English Reformation, primarily to be able to annul his marriage to Catherine of Aragon?

2. The plot of this 1985 novel takes place in an unnamed port city somewhere between the Caribbean Sea and the Magdalena river, and has Florentino Ariza and Fermina Daza as the main characters?

3. For whose death did the Belgian government issue a formal apology in 2002, admitting to a 'moral responsibility' and 'an irrefutable portion of responsibility in the events that led to the death'?

4. What institution, considered as the ultimate symbol of the Sultan's power, was guarded by a

small army of eunuchs, presided over by the Kizlar Aga or Chief Black Eunuch?

5. In which city do you find the red-light district called De Wallen, named so because of the walled canals created to avoid flooding of the local river?

6. Aphrodite, the Greek goddess of love, is considered to have been born off the coast of Cythera from the foam produced by whose genitals, which his son had severed and thrown into the sea?

7. The Enfield P53 rifle-musket introduced in India in 1856 was a contributing cause of the 1857 Indian war of Independence, due to rumors of its cartridges being greased with beef fat and pig tallow. Which British company, set up in the early 19th century in response to the Napoleonic War, developed this musket?

8. Which American executive, charged with manslaughter by Indian authorities following a major industrial incident, was portrayed by Martin Sheen in a movie based on the events?

9. Who, baptized under the name Rebecca and introduced to English society as an example of a 'civilized savage', was the subject of an Academy-award nominated animated film?

10. These are the last words of which famous literary character: "It is a far, far better thing that I do, than I have ever done; it is a far, far better rest that I go to than I have ever known."

11. Due to the controversial subject matter of this novel, its author originally intended to publish it under the pseudonym Vivian Darkbloom. Which novel was eventually published under the author's real name?

12. Which fictional character explains her name in the novel as coming from the Latin for 'evening', as she was born on a very stormy evening? She also lent her name to a popular drink after the novel's publication.

13. Which character, whose name has become a generic expression for a womanizer, is first referenced in the 1630 Spanish play 'The Trickster of Seville and the Stone Guest by Tirso de Molina?

14. Which Oscar-winning film was described on its cinematic poster as "In the harshest place on earth, love finds a way"?

Set 3

1. An effigy is created, typically using old clothes, newspapers and a mask. Notable people have been seen on effigies, including the likes of Paul Kruger and Margaret Thatcher. But this effigy, burnt every year on November 05, usually depicts which individual, remembering his role in events that happened on this date?

2. How do we better know Pope Alexander VI, who acknowledged fathering several children by his

mistresses, and whose surname became a byword for nepotism at the time?

3. Known locally as a kunik, it is a form of expressing affection. It is used by people when they meet outside, and due to the severe weather, have little exposed except their eyes and nose. How do we know this greeting better?

4. How do we collectively know Conrad Hilton Jr., Michael Wilding, Mike Todd, Eddie Fisher, Richard Burton, John Warner and Larry Fortensky?

5. Who, known for his investment scheme of paying earlier investors using the investments of later investors, taglined his autobiography as "The autobiography of a financial genius"?

6. In 2003, over 2.5 million books of this franchise were used in the preparation of the top layer of the West Midlands motorway in England. To quell the franchise's fans, a spokesman for the road contracting firm said, "We want to reassure readers that we're not just picking on their favorite books – other books are down there too." Name the franchise.

7. Which rock band is named after a 'revolutionary' steam-powered adult toy mentioned in the William S. Burroughs novel *Naked Lunch*?

8. Which 1970 best selling romance novel has influenced not just a successful Hollywood film, but also Indian remakes like *Ankhiyon Ke Jharokhon Se* and *Sanam Teri Kasam*?

9. What system, outlawed in India in 1988, was once supported by the Chola Empire, and involved (primarily) women dedicating themselves to worship and serve a deity or a temple for the rest of their lives?

10. The Great _____, considered as the greatest conman in Indian history, was known for repeatedly 'selling' the Taj Mahal and Red Fort among other monuments. Fill in the blanks with a name now synonymous with smart conmen in India.

11. No quiz on betrayals is complete without a question on Kim Philby. Which Frederick Forsyth novel features Philby getting involved in a plot to trigger a nuclear explosion in Britain?

12. What word, a portmanteau of the Greek words for 'I carry' and 'stimulating', refers to secreted chemicals which are capable of triggering a social response or behavioral change in members of the same species?

13. What Bollywood film, based on the Hollywood movie Lipstick, addressed the theme of rape and starred Zeenat Aman?

14. Which king of Gauda in Eastern Bengal, known better for his betrayal of the Vardhana dynasty, is often attributed with the development of the Bengali calendar, because its starting date falls within his reign?

2. SOLID, LIQUID, GAS

There are three states of matter, as my physics professor told me a long time ago in school. Enough said.

Set 1

1. For discovering what phenomenon was the Dutch physicist Heike Kamerlingh Onnes awarded the Nobel Prize in Physics in 1913?

2. Named after a former Soviet minister, what comprises a breakable glass bottle containing a flammable substance like petrol, with a burning cloth wick held in place by the bottle's stopper acting as a source of ignition?

3. What term was given to the group of 'tactical use' chemicals used by the US military during the Vietnam War? This group included, among others, Agent Orange.

4. What item, produced by the ancient Egyptians and Romans, came into its own as an art form in medieval Europe, when it became a pictorial form to illustrate Biblical narratives to the general populace?

5. Para-chloro-meta-xylenol (PCMX), first made in 1927, is an antiseptic and disinfectant used for skin disinfection and cleaning surgical instruments. It was initially planned to be sold as

PCMX, but this was thought to be a poor name. What was it renamed to? This also happens to be the most common brand name of this formulation today.

6. Widely considered as the 'father of modern chemistry', which chemist was charged with tax fraud during the French Revolution and guillotined?

7. In the Game of Thrones franchise, what substance, one of a few known to kill White Walkers, survived mainly as heirlooms in the noble houses of Westeros?

8. What, invented in 1815 for use in coal mines, consists of a wick lamp with the flame enclosed inside a mesh screen?

9. What liquid, used in potions and other useful mixtures, was used by Horace Slughorn to fake his own death in the book Harry Potter and the Half-Blood Prince?

10. What connects a Bing Crosby hit, a Marvel Comics superhero, an Irish quiz show and a chemical element?

11. Classified as a red supergiant and one of the largest stars visible to the naked eye, which star is known as Ardra in Sanskrit?

12. What dessert gets its name from its texture, which resembles the banks of one of the longest rivers in the world?

13. What drink, which commonly includes cherry liqueur, fresh lemon juice, soda and a type of alcohol, was developed by a Hainanese bartender in the early 20th century?

14. If Jupiter is known for the Great Red Spot, which extraterrestrial body is known for the Great Dark Spot?

Set 2

1. What term more commonly used in the business world is used to refer to a coarse-grained sedimentary rock, which is formed by the consolidation and lithification of gravel?

2. These geographical features are found at high altitudes and high latitudes. They create debris which ranges from large boulders to small dust. What is this debris called, a word derived from the Franco-Provencal dialect meaning snout?

3. Thomas Jennings was an abolitionist and the first African American to be awarded a patent in 1821. What was he awarded the patent for? The process most commonly uses a liquid called perchloroethylene.

4. They were (supposedly) first shown at the Paris Motor Show in 1910. They grew in popularity until, in 1919, the Paris Opera entrance used them. They were introduced to the USA in 1923 and soon became popular. What items, have been seen, among other places, in Times Square?

5. This condition was first demonstrated by Robert Boyle in 1670. It came to be called caisson disease in the 1850s, because many caisson workers at the Royal Albert Bridge reported it. What condition involves dissolved gases coming out of solution into bubbles?

6. This ale blue liquid is slightly more viscous than water and is used as a bleaching agent and antiseptic. In a concentrated form it is used as a rocket propellant. What compound is this, which is naturally unstable in light and is thus stored in dark colored bottles?

7. This substance is used in a variety of items around us. It has no nutritional energy and a metallic aftertaste. What is this substance, which most of us would have consumed at some point, and whose common scientific name is benzoic sulfimide?

8. In its most well-known form, it is a green, crystalline material. Other varieties like red and gold have also come up over time. What material is this, which has become synonymous with 'Achilles heel' due to its effects on a very popular person?

9. What term meaning 'nectar of the gods' is also the name of a very popular brand of Indian whisky? The company however translates the name as 'elixir of life'.

10. In Greek mythology, it was thought to be the pure essence that the gods breathed. In early science, it

came to denote the material that fills the universe above the terrestrial sphere. It was used to explain several natural phenomena such as gravity and the travel of light. What's the good word?

11. Particulate matter in the air is a serious risk to health. Such particulates are typically denoted using the notation $PM_{2.5}$ or PM_{10}. What do the subscripts signify?

12. This is considered to be a miraculously generated source of water from God, which sprang when Ibrahim's son Ismail and his mother Hajar were thirsty in the desert. What, located 20 meters east of the Kaaba?

13. What material, named after one of the protagonists in an HG Wells novel, could negate the forces of gravity? It is also later used by an antagonist in the graphic novel 'The League of Extraordinary Gentlemen'.

14. Considered the world's first offshore oil platform, is also a functional city with over 300 km of streets built on piles of dirt and landfill. This settlement, called Oily Rocks in the local language, is a township in which national capital?

Set 3

1. Known for his achievements in optics and the field of gravitation, what topic is said to have comprised nearly 10% of his written works? Some of the content would likely have been considered heretical by the church at the time.

2. In the wake of World War I, this German company had to shut down and surrender all its assets under the terms of the Treaty of Versailles. One exception was made, to build an item for the US Navy, and this saved the company from extinction. What item did they make that continued to be popular until 1937?

3. It was first known to be built under the orders of Empress Anna, as part of the celebrations of Russia's victory over the Ottoman Empire. Many more have been built since then. Now they serve as tourist attractions or destination hotels. What am I talking about?

4. Extraction typically happens only from May to August, when this item can be removed from the tree without causing permanent damage. About half of this item is made in Portugal. What item is this, whose near impermeability makes it suitable for use in something a lot of us are familiar with?

5. What generic term is used to describe fog, mist, dust, geyser steam and smoke, all with particles having a diameter less than $1\,\mu m$?

6. In folklore, this was seen by travellers at night, especially over swamps or marshes, and was said

to mislead them. In literature, it has come to mean hope or a goal that leads one on but is impossible to reach. What is this, which modern science attributes to oxidation of phosphine, diphosphane and methane?

7. This colorless and odorless compound is chemically known as (RS)-propan-2-yl methyl-phosphono-fluoridate. It is extremely toxic and can cause suffocation from lung muscle paralysis in case a lethal dose is ingested, and neurological damage in the case of a non-lethal dose. What compound is this, famously used in a terrorist attack on a subway?

8. What substance, which gains energy on striking a hard surface, was invented by Professor Brainard in the 1961 movie 'The Absent-Minded Professor'?

9. Where do you mind these items in this particular order: Talc, Gypsum, Calcite, Fluorite, Apatite, Orthoclase feldspar, Quartz, Topaz, Corundum, Diamond?

10. The word comes from the Italian meaning 'an empty space or gap'. It evolved into a more recent form while describing the area around Venice. What is this English word which is also a common geographical feature?

11. Mayonnaise, foam over coffee and vinaigrette are common examples of what mixture, made of 2 or more liquids that are normally immiscible?

12. This term has been used to refer to any substance that is needed to build some device critical to the plot of a science fiction story, but which does not exist in the universe as we know it. In the movie Avatar, it is mined on the moon, Pandora. What substance is this?

13. Most popular for their role in refrigerants, what chemical compounds have been phased out under the Montreal Protocol due to their impact on the ozone layer?

14. Until the early 20th century, this was sold without a prescription and was a constituent of many patent medicines. Today it is recognized as addictive and strictly regulated. What substance, which features in multiple novels such as Wilkie Collins' *The Moonstone*, Mary Shelley's *Frankenstein* and Charles Dickens' *Oliver Twist*. It also features in the Asterix comics and is named in every Asterix comic.

3. ROTI, KAPDA, MAKAAN

This iconic phrase meaning 'Food, Clothing and Shelter' was popularized in the late 1960s by the former Prime Minister of India, Indira Gandhi. It is also the name of an iconic 1974 Bollywood film directed by Manoj Kumar. This set of questions is being compiled while I am under lockdown due to COVID-19, so it made sense to stick to the essentials.

Set 1

1. This two-piece suit was prepared at a cost of ₹10 lakh, and later sold for a world record auction price of ₹4.3 crores. Who was it designed for, a name you couldn't have missed if you have seen the suit?

2. What building am I talking about when I say it has 27 floors, 3 helipads, a 168-car garage, a ballroom, an 80-seat theater, terrace gardens, a spa, a temple and accommodation for 600 staff?

3. What item is featured on the royal flag of the princely state of Hyderabad? According to legend, Asaf Jah visited a Sufi holy man who shared his meal with him. Asaf Jah ate seven of these items, and the holy man then blessed him saying his descendants would rule the Deccan for several generations.

4. What dessert was invented in the last decade of the 19th century by French chef Auguste Escoffier at the Savoy Hotel, London, in honor of a performer at the opera?

5. What resulted when Hermes chief executive Jean-Louis Dumas was seated next to an actress on a flight, and she explained to him how she found it hard to find a leather bag she liked?

6. What was designed by architect James Hoban and is located at 1600 Pennsylvania Avenue?

7. And what is located at 2 Bhausaheb Hirey Marg in Mumbai? It was built in 1936, was used for 10 years by its original owner, and has recently been at the center of an ownership dispute.

8. This classic comfort food consists of a clear broth, often with pieces of meat or vegetables. It also features in the title of a very popular self-help book series. What is it?

9. The first Ironman suit was made using ordinary iron and was centered around an iron chest plate designed to prevent shrapnel from reaching Tony Stark's heart and killing him. In the 2008 film, he uses it to escape from captors in Afghanistan. Which country does he escape from in the comics?

10. Under the Bureau of Indian Standards (BIS), what is specified in Standard IS1 under the section TXD8?

11. What item, whose name means 'mountain of light', is currently owned by the British Royal family? It has been used only by female members of the royal family because it had a reputation of bringing bad luck to any man who wears it.

12. What architectural feature came into use in Catholic houses of England, after Queen Elizabeth I came to the throne in 1558 and severe measures were taken against Catholics?

13. What Spanish word for sauce, which derives from the Latin word for 'salted', is now commonly used to refer to condiments served with Mexican cuisine?

14. What was created when Joe Gebbia and Brian Chesky put an air mattress in their living room in San Francisco in 2007 and offered it as short-term living quarters?

Set 2

1. The edible species of the red algae genus Pyropia has a strong and distinctive flavor. It is processed and sold in the form of dried sheets. What is it most commonly used for? You will find it in Japanese restaurants.

2. Which street, built in the 1730s, previously held the headquarters of the Royal Geographical Society, but has been known since the 19th century for a particular occupation? It also features in a popular 2014 spy movie.

3. What fictional realm, based on Norse mythology, is home to several characters from the Marvel Comics universe?

4. Why did Treetops Hotel, located near the township of Nyeri in Kenya, become famous around the world in February 1952?

5. Which film follows the protagonist's efforts to get to Paradise Falls to complete a promise made to his late wife? And how does he get there?

6. What family of polymers was developed by DuPont and is apocryphally considered to be named after 2 major cities on either side of the Atlantic?

7. What rice dish gets its name from the local word for 'frying pan', due to the wide and shallow traditional pan that is used to cook the dish on an open fire?

8. Derived from a Celtic word meaning 'border', which Scottish river is associated with a fabric, an icon of Scottish clothing?

9. What street dish, originating from Kolkata in West Bengal, India, is named after the sticks used to skewer and cook the meat used in the dish?

10. What dish does Peter Clemenza teach Michael Corleone how to make in the movie 'The Godfather'?

11. What type of fermented, cured and smoked sausage, popular in Goa, India, gets its smokiness and deep red color from dried red chillies?

12. What extremely expensive (and now banned) item is named from the Persian 'king of fine wools'?

13. Name India's first scientific base station in Antarctica, built in 1984 and decommissioned in 1990.

14. Where was the royal family of England believed to be residing during World War II, for morale and propaganda purposes? And where did they actually live during the war?

Set 3

1. This traditional Louisiana sandwich is usually made with fried seafood. A popular local theory says it got its name during a 1929 strike by streetcar conductors. The workers at the restaurant making this sandwich called the strikers by this term, which then got shortened due to the Louisiana dialect. What sandwich is this?

2. We spoke about the ultra-expensive two-piece suit made for Indian Prime Minister Narendra Modi. Which former princely state did this type of suit originate from?

3. What hand-made embroidery style from India is most popularly credited to Mughal Empress Noor Jahan, who is believed to have introduced the style to India? If you know the answer, you're in luck now.

4. What iconic restaurant in the French quarter of New Orleans featured prominently in the 2014 Jon Favreau film 'Chef'?

5. What building material made from earth and organic materials like dung or straw, has come to mean any kind of earthen construction in several English-speaking regions of Spanish heritage? This is something you would come across in the deserts of the Western world.

6. And what portable tent is typically carried on camel or yak backs, takes 2 hours to construct, and is named after the **Turkic** for the imprint it leaves in the ground?

7. What item of Indian clothing first emerged during the Non-Cooperation movement of 1918-21, remained popular until the early years of independent India, and then saw a resurgence in the 2010s? The person it is named after seems to have worn it only for a couple of years.

8. What popular food item associated with France is often used to describe the dosa from South India in Indian restaurants in the western world?

9. This very popular picnic food in the United Kingdom has several theories about its origin. The Oxford dictionary first mentions it in 1809 as a dinner dish, served hot with gravy. A London department store popularized them in the 1730s (and claims to have invented them as well as a traveller's snack). It is also believed to have

derived from a Mughlai dish called Nargisikofta. What is the food?

10. This item of clothing is attributed to Catherine de Medici, queen of France, who banned thick waists at court in the 1550s. The item remained in fashion until the 1920s, when easier to use alternatives emerged. It has seen brief revivals in the fashion industry, most famously in 2001 and coinciding with the release of the movie 'Moulin Rouge'. What item?

11. In igloos, what item serves to insulate the structure? A tunnel is also used to reduce wind and heat loss when opening the door.

12. The other end of the spectrum from question 1 of this set. The recipe calls for oysters topped with a rich sauce of butter, parsley, herbs and breadcrumbs. This New Orleans dish was named after a famous person due to its ingredients, and the name stuck. What is the dish?

13. What iconic sporting venue known for an annual event with a strict dress code, and also known for the hats patrons wear at the event, prominently features in the movie 'My Fair Lady'?

14. What name is shared by the fictional dwellings of Charles Foster Kane and Mandrake the Magician? It is also the nickname for the real house of Bill Gates.

4. GERMANY, ITALY, JAPAN

The villains of World War II, Germany, Italy and Japan formed an alliance that fought a global war for six years. The war was lost, but a timeless trio was born.

Set 1

1. The BMW logo is often thought to be the portrayal of an aircraft propeller with white blades cutting across a blue sky. But why does the logo actually have these specific colors?

2. The ancient Roman historian Tacitus is known for his *Annals* & *Histories*, separate works which span the history of the Roman Empire. They cover the period from whose death in 14 AD, to the first Jewish-Roman war in 70 AD?

3. Which samurai is credited with saving the life of Tokugawa Ieyasu and helping him become the ruler of united Japan? He appears a lot in popular culture, including as a prominent swordsmith in an early 2000's movie.

4. Who is the only member of the Nazi Party to have been honored with a burial in Jerusalem on Mount Zion?

5. The medieval Italian scholar Petrarch's rediscovery of whose letters is often credited with initiating the 14ᵗʰ century Italian Renaissance?

6. By what name is the period from 1603 to 1868, when Japan was under the rule of the Tokugawa Shogunate, known? It was named after a castle town, a former fishing village that grew into a metropolis under the Shogunate.

7. What popular tourist attraction was named after a statue of Nero that once stood nearby? The statue no longer stands, but the attraction, while ruined, continues to attract tourists.

8. Douglas Douglas-Hamilton, the 14th Duke of Hamilton, was one of the first men to fly over Mount Everest. What 1941 event brought him into brief prominence during World War II?

9. The Gutenberg Bible, one of the first major printed books, was printed by Johannes Gutenberg in Germany in the 1450s. What is it also known as, a reference to the number of printed lines on each page of the Bible?

10. What is the former name of Lushunkou District, located in the Liaodong Peninsula of China and possessing an excellent natural harbor? Its possession was one of the reasons leading to the Russo-Japanese War in 1904-05.

11. 30 April 2019 was the last day of Heisei 31, and 01 May 2019 was the first day of Reiwa 1. What am I talking about?

12. The former Roman cities of Sabratha & Leptis Magna, both with well-preserved ruins, are located in which modern-day country, which sees tourism contributing only a small percentage of its GDP?

13. What historical character, remembered primarily for his surrender after losing a battle in 52 BC, is considered a folk hero in the Auvergne region of France?

14. According to Japanese chronology, which goddess, whose name means "shining in heaven" are the Emperors of Japan considered to be direct descendants of?

Set 2

1. Which German city is known for the protestation by Lutheran princes in 1529, against an edict condemning the teachings of Martin Luther as heretical?

2. Which king appointed Benito Mussolini as Prime Minister, thus transferring political power to the fascists after their March on Rome in October 1922?

3. The name of which irregular army supposedly came about when their exiled leader, in 1843, used clothing from a stock destined for slaughterhouse workers in Buenos Aires?

4. Which former German colony, made a League of Nations mandate after World War I, was then ruled by a former British colony until its independence in 1990?

5. What was opened on 22 March 1933, in an unused gunpowder and munitions factory to hold prisoners in protective custody?

6. What animal, often mistaken for the western badger or raccoon, plays a prominent role in Japanese folklore and is known for being a master of disguise and shapeshifting?

7. They are always twice as long as wide, and broadly have three sizes, differing across the Kyoto, Nagoya and Tokyo regions. The name means to fold or pile. What am I talking about?

8. The German conglomerate IG Farben was formed in 1925 from the merger of Bayer, Hoechst, Agfa, Chemische Fabrik Griesheim-Elektron, Chemische Fabrikvorm & which other company?

9. Italy's second-oldest university, and known to have existed as early as 1222, counted among its attendees' such names as Nicolaus Copernicus and William Harvey. Galileo Galilei was a faculty member there. Which city will you find it in?

10. This art form is said to originate in 12th century scrolls. The word, meaning 'whimsical pictures', is commonly recorded in 1798. The post-World War II period saw an explosion of creative activity. What is this art form which is now a multi-million-dollar industry?

11. The 1966 flooding of the river Arno caused widespread damage to art and masterpieces in which city? The *Magdalene Penitent* sculpture by Donatello was, among many other items, damaged, leading to restoration efforts that continued for decades.

12. Which German physicist and engineer won the first Nobel Prize in Physics in 1901, and has element 111 named after him?

13. What first appeared on 27 October 1954, and has reappeared 36 times since, being recognized by the Guinness Book of World Records for its longevity?

14. Which of Albert Einstein's friends helped him with his lecture notes at Zurich Polytechnic, as well in getting a job at the Swiss Patent office in Bern?

Set 3

1. The country was known for its mercenaries in the medieval period, peaking during the Renaissance due to their proven battlefield capabilities. Eventually, the country's military isolationism ended mercenary activity, and now only one group remains. Which country is this? And what is the surviving group?

2. Who debuted in the 1947 film *Snow Trail*, before coming to prominence in the 1948 Akira Kurosawa film *Drunken Angel*?

3. Ken Watanabe & Ryan Phillippe played lead roles in which pair of films released in 2006? They were based on the same event.

4. The name of this Italian province comes from the original primitive footwear of its inhabitants, called *ciocie*. It was subject to war atrocities by the

Moroccan Goumiers after the Battle of Monte Cassino in World War II. What Academy Award-winning film was based on these events?

5. What started when Crown Prince Ludwig married Princess Therese on 12 October 1810 and all the citizens of the town were invited to attend the festivities held on the fields in front of the city gates?

6. Which influential German philosopher was commonly believed to have never travelled more than 16 kilometers from his home town of Konigsberg throughout his life?

7. Boiled sausages such as the type used in North American hot dogs are commonly called frankfurters, including in Austria where they were supposedly brought by a Frankfurt butcher. What are they called in Germany?

8. Born in San Francisco to a Japanese father and American Caucasian mother, which fictional amateur sleuth living in Tokyo features in a series of mystery novels written by Sujata Massey?

9. The *nuraghe*is a type of ancient megalithic edifice, with over 7,000 structures found. They are believed to have been built between 1800 and 1200 BC by a civilization that left behind no written records. Where would you go to see the *nuragheis*?

10. The 16th century Chinese novel *Journey to the West* is an account of a Buddhist monk who travels to the 'Western Regions' to obtain sacred Buddhist

texts and returns after many trials. Which Japanese media franchise did it inspire?

11. Which Leonardo da Vinci painting, rediscovered and restored in the early 21st century, set a then record for the most expensive painting ever sold at a public auction, selling for $450.3 million in 2017?

12. The Ryukyuan people are an East Asia ethnic group native to the Ryukyu Islands. Now part of Japan, these people are now found in 2 prefectures. One is Kagoshima, which is the other?

13. The Mighty Magyars, as the Hungary national football team of the 1950s was known, is widely regarded as one of the best international football teams ever. It recorded 42 victories, 7 draws and just 1 defeat in the years from 1950-1956. Who was the defeat to?

14. The abbreviated phrase SPQR stands for 'Senatus Populus Que Romanus' meaning 'The Roman Senate & People'. A humorous expansion has been used in Italy 'Sono Pazzi Questi Romani', a phrase you would also see in a series of French comic books. What does the humorous expansion mean?

5. ARMY, NAVY, AIR FORCE

Land, water and air – the three known spheres of warfare at the time of writing this question set. A lot of our history has focused on wars and creating sets of questions using this trio which has played such a key role in wars was the logical next step.

Set 1

1. How do we better know the USS Diablo, which served in the US Navy from 1945 to 1963, and was then loaned to, and eventually procured by, the Navy of another country?

2. Which ancient Indian king is mentioned in the Rig Veda as leading his tribe to victory in the Battle of the Ten Kings, establishing the ascendancy of the Bharata clan?

3. Carlo Piazza was the first person to accomplish what feat, on 23 October 1911, during the Libyan War between Italy and Turkey?

4. In the Mahabharata, what was the battle formation consisting of 21,870 chariots, 21,870 elephants, 65,610 horses and 109,350 infantry called?

5. What fort, first built during the reign of Raja Bhoja II of the Shilahar dynasty and rebuilt by Shivaji Maharaj, was established by Maratha

Admiral Kanhoji Angre has his capital along the coast?

6. The Enola Gay bomber is known for dropping the first atomic bomb on the city of Hiroshima. Which bomber dropped the second one on Nagasaki?

7. Which British flying ace was known for losing his legs in a crash in 1931, and subsequently rejoining the Royal Air Force in World War II and winning notable victories until his capture in 1941?

8. Which city is associated with Operation Thunderbolt, also sometimes referred to as Operation Jonathan in memory of the unit's leader Yonatan Netanyahu?

9. Which general serving the Adil Shah Sultanate of Bijapurwas defeated by Shivaji Maharaj at the Battle of Pratapgad in 1659?

10. Which South East Asian empire, dated from the 7th to the 12th century AD, was invaded by the navy of the Chola Empire of South India?

11. Which 1415 battle of the Hundred Years War featured an unexpected English victory over a numerically superior French army? It was notable for the use of the English longbow and features prominently in the Shakespeare play *Henry V*.

12. Name the first aircraft carrier of the Indian Navy, which was in active service from 1961 to 1997, and was preserved as a museum ship until 2012 before being scrapped.

13. And what motorbike launched by Bajaj Auto in 2016 was built using metal from the aircraft carrier mentioned in the previous question?

14. The 1937 bombing of which city inspired, among other things, a woodcut by Heinz Kiwitz, a painting by Rene Magritte, a sculpture by Rene Iche and a musical composition by Octavio Vazquez? It is most famously depicted in a Pablo Picasso painting.

Set 2

1. What collection, dating from the 3rd century BC, was discovered on 29 March 1974 by local farmers of Lintong District, who were trying to dig a water well?

2. The popular fictional character Jack Ryan made his first appearance in which 1984 Tom Clancy novel, set in large part in a naval setting?

3. What mixture, which burns at temperatures ranging from 800 to 1200 degrees Centigrade, was first developed in 1942? Its name is a portmanteau of the names of two of its original constituents, naphthenic acid and palmitic acid.

4. The Battle of Thermopylae between Sparta and the Persian Empire is known for its stand of 300 Spartans guarding the narrow pass against the Persian Army. Which Greek traitor is believed to have given away the route of a small goat path to the Persians, allowing them to outflank and defeat the Spartans?

5. And where was a subsequent naval battle fought between a Greek city-state alliance and the Persian Empire, leading to a Persian retreat back to Asia?

6. He was born to a Prussian aristocratic family in 1892 and entitled to a title of nobility. This combined with his preferred colors in combat is believed to have led to his most common moniker. Who am I talking about who is a World War I hero with over 80 recorded victories?

7. Its modern version is believed to have originated in the 1660s when mercenaries of a specific country were enlisted by Louis XIV of France. Their military kit included an item that aroused Parisian curiosity. This item then entered popular fashion, named after the mercenaries, or rather the country they came from. What item is this?

8. And what name was given to an irregular soldier of the Ottoman Army, mostly recruited from among Albanians and Circassians? These units had a reputation for bravery but were undisciplined. The term meant 'one whose head is turned' and became popular as an expletive often used by Captain Haddock in *The Adventures of Tintin*.

9. What decisive naval battle from the last years of the Han Dynasty was immortalized in a 2008 John Woo film? The exact location of the battle has renamed a topic for scholarly debate till date.

10. What name, more commonly seen in an individual ball sport, was given to the operation

undertaken by United Nations peacekeeping forces (which included Indian soldiers as well) against the State of Katanga, a secessionist state rebelling against the Republic of the Congo?

11. What military decoration was established during the Napoleonic Wars by King Friedrich Wilhelm III of Prussia? The design was black with a white or silver outline, derived from a sign worn by knights of the Teutonic Order in the 13th century. It featured the Swastika at the center during World War II and was reintroduced after the war only in 1956.

12. What ship, launched by the Cunard Line in 1906 and known for a while for the fastest Atlantic crossing, was sunk by German U-boats in 1915? It shared its name with an ancient Roman province that covers modern Portugal and parts of Western Spain.

13. Name the first Indian-developed jet aircraft, also the first Asian jet fighter to go into successful production and active service. It first flew in 1961 and was delivered to the Indian Air Force in 1967.

14. What code name was given to the operation by the Indian Peace Keeping Force (IPKF) to take control of Jaffna from the Liberation Tigers of Tamil Eelam (LTTE) in late 1987, as part of the Indo-Sri Lanka Accord?

Set 3

1. What conflict lasted 74 days, and involved a war over a set of islands & its territorial dependencies, South Georgia and the South Sandwich Islands?

2. The first Indian circumnavigation of the globe was undertaken from 1985 to 1987, by an Indian Army Corps of Engineers. Name the yacht they sailed on which saw a place in honor in the Republic Day parade the following year.

3. This term meaning 'divine wind' originated in the 13th century, to refer to the major typhoons which dispersed Kublai Khan's fleets and prevented them from invading this country. The name was then used in 1937 to describe a monoplane which flew from the country's capital to London. The most common use of the term is from World War II to describe certain special attack units of the country's air force. What is the term?

4. The word derives from French and literally means 'holding a position'. It originally meant someone who was a placeholder for a superior during the latter's absence. Which army rank is this, notable for being pronounced differently on either side of the Atlantic even though the spelling is the same?

5. What branch of the Indian Army has a prerequisite of gainful employment or self-employment in a civil profession for people who want to join it? Notable members include politicians Sachin Pilot and Anurag Thakur, and cricketers Kapil Dev and Mahendra Singh Dhoni.

6. Name this English sea captain who, among other things, carried out a circumnavigation of the world in a single expedition, was knighted, claimed what is now California for the English, and was branded as a pirate by the Spanish due to his privateering?

7. What 1982 Bollywood film starring, among others, Rekha, Shashi Kapoor and Amrish Puri, is notable for showing aerial photography of active Indian Air Force aircraft of the 1980s?

8. What cult Bollywood film features the protagonist Karan Shergill, who joins and graduates from the Indian Military Academy, and then joins the 3rd battalion of the Punjab Regiment in Kargil, and finally secures Point 5179 during the Kargil War?

9. Which head of state was assassinated on 06 October 1981, during an annual victory parade to celebrate a key operation the country undertook during the Yom Kippur War?

10. What South African province was named by Portuguese explorer Vasco da Gama when he passed its coastline on Christmas Day 1497, on the course of his historic journey to India?

11. How do we better know the Unites States Navy Strike Fighter Tactics Instructor program, established in 1969 at the Naval Air Station in San Diego, California, in response to a high aircraft casualty rate during the Vietnam War?

12. What commercially successful 1991 Hollywood film was a parody of a film based on the previous

question, and starred, among others, Jon Cryer, Kristy Swanson and Cary Elwes?

13. The original structure was built in 1696 by the British East India Company, with permission granted by the Mughal Emperor Aurangzeb. It was attacked in 1756 and taken over, leading the British to build a new fort, which evolved into a now iconic structure. What structure is this? It is named after a monarch and now the property of the Indian Army.

14. This ship of the British Navy conducted three major voyages. In the first, it sailed to South America and back. In the third, it surveyed large parts of Australia. Who was its most famous passenger when it circumnavigated the world in its second voyage from 1831-36?

6. AGRICULTURE, INDUSTRY, SERVICES

The three-sector model of economics is something we all have used to talk about the three types of economic activity. This model has extended to describe countries economically as well. And this set of economic sectors forms our next trio.

Set 1

1. What Neolithic site, now located near the Bolan Pass near the Pakistani city of Quetta and discovered in 1974, is now seen as a precursor to the Indus Valley Civilization? It is also considered to be one of the earliest sites of farming in South Asia.

2. The descendants of which town of India consider themselves, per Indian mythology, as the descendants of Sage Markanda, the master weaver of the gods who is believed to have woven tissue from lotus fiber? It's a popular handloom hub known for the wide borders of its products.

3. What term has recently come to refer to the ability of a business, using a computing platform, to facilitate peer-to-peer transactions between clients and providers of a service, often bypassing the role of centrally planned companies? It refers

to a firm founded in 2009 which played a pioneering role in this space.

4. What business profession, which focuses on measuring and analyzing the risk of financial security systems, including their complexity, mathematics and mechanisms, has been consistently rated one of the most desirable professions worldwide in the 2010s?

5. The ancient Roman collegium, or corpus, was an organized group of people specialized in a specific activity, and whose membership of the group was voluntary. These groups didn't survive the collapse of the Roman Empire but sprang up again in medieval Europe. What specific word is used to refer to such a group?

6. What was set up by the conservationist Cary Fowler on the island of Spitsbergen, as an attempt to preserve and protect a wide variety of seeds from other gene banks worldwide?

7. What term is used to collectively describe the following food items, now found all over the world maize, peanut, potato, pineapple, blueberry, squash, tomato, and cashew? Note that the list is not exhaustive.

8. The moving line innovation reduced production time for a single unit from 12.5 man-hours to 1.5 man-hours. This made paint a bottleneck, and the Japan black paint was the only color that dried fast enough. What did this lead to, something which lasted from 1914 to 1926?

9. This term was first coined in 2007 by opponents, who intended it as a pejorative. By 2012, even supporters were using it. What are we talking about, which was signed into law in 2010 and is known as the Patient Protection and Affordable Care Act?

10. What started off as a prototype service in Aachen in 1850 using homing pigeons and then electric telegraphy? The founder then moved to London in 1851 and started a news wire agency, building a reputation as the first to report news from around the world?

11. What was constructed between 1898 and 1903, significantly reducing the time needed for the then government to move from its winter to summer capitals and then back? The earlier move required horses and ox-drawn carts.

12. What term is used to describe a series of research and technology initiatives in the 1950s and 60s, and was first used in a speech in 1968 by William Gaud, the administrator of the US Agency for International Development (USAID)?

13. From which country did the United Kingdom import cotton during the 1860s, to cover for shortfalls from the US cotton industry, the latter having been impacted by the American Civil War? The country in question was known for the quality of its textiles across history but had been reduced to just a cotton producer over time by the colonial government.

14. What compound, first synthesized in 1874, won Paul Muller a Nobel Prize in Medicine in 1948 for the discovery of its use as a poison against arthropods? It was available for public use from 1945 and was banned by 1972 due to the discovery of its environmental impact.

Set 2

1. What academic institution was founded in 1885 by US Senator Leland _____ & his wife Jane, in memory of their only child Leland Jr., who had died of typhoid fever the previous year?

2. And which Indian academic institution is set up on the site of a former British-era detention camp? The camp was last used in 1942, while the institution was set up in 1951.

3. What multinational group was founded in 1943 by then 17-year old Ingvar Kamprad, who was born on his family farm called Elmtaryd, near the village Agunnaryd?

4. Most plants of the legume family are used extensively in crop rotation because they help soil nutrient replenishment through what chemical process?

5. How do we commonly know the irregularly recurring flow of unusually warm surface waters, toward and along the western coast of South America, preventing the upwelling of nutrient-rich cold deep water? Something of great interest to farmers of the Indian subcontinent.

6. What method, employing single-sized crushed stone layers of small stones compacted thoroughly, was first used at Marsh Road near Bristol, England in 1816? It turned out to be a huge improvement over the prevailing method of employing large stones in the foundation.

7. What song, written in 1954 by Woody Guthrie but never recorded, talks about the alleged racist housing practices of his Brooklyn apartment landlord? The song was unearthed and put to music in 2016.

8. What hospital chain in India was founded by Dr. Venkataswamy in 1976? He wanted to emulate the service efficiency of McDonald's fast-food chains, to cope with the rising number of patients waiting to be treated.

9. What inventor, known for his role in the British Agricultural Revolution, perfected a horse-drawn seed drill in 1700 that sowed seeds in neat rows? Rock music fans will be familiar with the name.

10. Ronald Wayne sold, for $800, 10% of his shares in which company on 12 April 1976?

11. Which 1937 classic by George Orwell documents his experiences living in the bleak living conditions of the Lancashire and Yorkshire working class in the industrial north of England?

12. The Bonvoy loyalty program of the Marriott hotels was formed through the 2019 merger of three reward programs – Marriott Rewards, Ritz-Carlton Rewards and which third program?

13. Which Academy award-nominated movie tells the tale of a pig raised as livestock who wants to do the work of a sheepdog?

14. Through the issuance of bonds and shares of stock to the general public, which became the world's first formally listed public company in the early 1600s?

Set 3

1. In ancient Egypt, the god Hapi, typically depicted as an androgynous figure with a big belly and large drooping breasts, wearing a loincloth and ceremonial false beard, was the personification of what?

2. Who, in 1929, was the first partner hired by the consulting firm James O. McKinsey and Company? He was managing director of their Chicago office when it split from the rest of the company in 1939.

3. What was founded on 01 September 1956, through the nationalization of over 245 companies? Its slogan translates to "Your welfare is our responsibility" in English.

4. Which Augustinian friar and abbot has been posthumously recognized for his pea plant experiments conducted between 1856 and 1863?

5. Which seaport, the second largest on the continent, was first set up in 1811 when Napoleon Bonaparte recognized its potential and ordered the construction of its first lock?

6. What commonly used horticultural technique is recorded, among other places, in the Old Testament and in Jia Sixie's 6th century CE Chinese treatise 'Essential Skills for the Common People'? In Europe, it was used in the Roman Empire but then survived only in Christian monasteries until the Renaissance.

7. What distinctively colored compound was supplied from India to Europe as early as the Greco-Roman era, influencing the name of the compound as well? It also became popular in Japan during the Edo period and had a high value as a trading commodity throughout history.

8. Whose first startup was a company called Softronics which failed in the 1970s? He did much better with his second attempt launched in 1981 with six others.

9. Comcast's intention to buy which company in 2014 for around $45.2 billion was eventually withdrawn, following a Department of Justice attempt to file an antitrust lawsuit to block the sale?

10. Its name derives from its similarity to stone quarried on an island in Dorset, England. It was patented in 1824 and takes the form of a fine powder, produced by heating limestone and clay minerals in a kiln, which is then ground and mixed with 2 to 3 percent of gypsum.

11. Blight infecting which crops was considered as the cause of the Great Famine of Ireland from 1845 to 1849?

12. Flint corn, pod corn, popcorn, flour corn, sweet corn and dent corn are the six major types of which grain, a staple food in many parts of the world and a key ingredient in ethanol and other biofuels?

13. Which company, founded as a gunpowder mill in 1802, is known for developing, among other things, Freon, Lycra and Teflon?

14. The last naturally occurring cases of what was diagnosed in Somalia in October 1977 and in Bangladesh in October 1975?

7. PAST, PRESENT, FUTURE

The three-time references we were taught in grammar school. Events that have happened, are happening and will (or should I say, might) happen. Our next trio: this was, is and will be.

Set 1

1. What was discovered in 1901 at the ancient site of Susa, in present day Iran, by Egyptologist Gustave Jequier? It had 244 items in the Cuneiform script, arranged in 44 columns and 28 paragraphs.

2. In 1926, two years after Veer Savarkar was released from prison, his biography was published, titled "Life of Barrister Savarkar" and authored by someone called 'Chitragupta'. Who was Chitragupta revealed to be, in the 1987 edition of the book?

3. What English term, often used to describe the Day of Judgment of Abrahamic religions, refers to the blast of trumpets signalling the end of the world? The term was famously used by William Shakespeare in Macbeth as well.

4. What was the then English Premier League chairman Richard Scudamore talking about when he said, "If this was a once in every 5,000-year

event, then we've effectively got another 5,000 years of hope ahead of us?"

5. The massive rock temples of Abu Simbel in Egypt were built in the 13th century BC during the reign of the Pharaoh Rameses II and show four big rock statues. Who do the statues depict?

6. Whose supporters retrospectively claim that he predicted major world events, such as the Great Fire of London, the French Revolution, the atomic bombings of Hiroshima and Nagasaki, the September 11 attacks, and most recently the 2019 Coronavirus outbreak?

7. What hypothetical particles, considered to travel faster than light, are commonly used in fiction, limiting Dr. Manhattan's ability to see into the future in the graphic novel series Watchmen, and powering a device that can see the past and the future in the Hollywood film *Tomorrowland*?

8. The Indian cricket team captain Virat Kohli has been prolific in One Day Internationals. However, by his usual high standards, he had a lean 2019 World Cup, with no hundreds across 9 innings. When was the last time he went 7 innings without a hundred?

9. Whose capture and subsequent execution of the emperor Atahualpa in 1532 eventually led to the Spanish conquest of Peru?

10. What was surveyed between 1763 and 1767 to resolve a border dispute between the colonial states of Maryland, Pennsylvania and Delaware? It

is more popularly known in the context of the American Civil War.

11. The Berlin Wall was brought down in 1989 but some portions still stand. The standing portions are covered in a lot of graffiti, but what is the key difference between graffiti seen on the Wall when it stood before 1989, and after it was brought down?

12. The Batman one-shot special "Ghosts", written by Jeph Loeb, has Bruce Wayne visited by three spirits, in the form of Poison Ivy, the Joker and the Grim Reaper, giving him a message to not let Batman take over his entire life. What classic of English literature is this special based on?

13. What is common to the US states of North Carolina, South Carolina, Virginia, West Virginia, Maryland, Louisiana and Georgia?

14. Which record-breaking football World Cup scorer was substituted for Mario Gotze in the 88th minute of the 2014 Football World Cup final against Argentina, with Gotze going on to score the winning goal in the 113th minute?

Set 2

1. What artistic movement, founded in Milan in 1909, expressed a loathing of everything old, especially political and artistic tradition? The movement glorified modernity and aimed to liberate Italy from the weight of its past. It also

spurred parallel movements in other countries, especially in Portugal and Russia.

2. Which English natural philosopher, known for coining the term 'cell' and for his work in microscopy and map-making, is best remembered for his disputes with Isaac Newton, and for a law of physics named after him?

3. The Chinese pharmaceutical chemist Tu Youyou won the 2015 Nobel Prize in Medicine for her discoveries in treating which infectious disease, which caused over 400,000 deaths in 2018?

4. Which fictional family resides in Skypad apartments in Orbit City, where people commute in aerocars with transparent bubble tops?

5. Which great-great-granddaughter of the celebrated seer Cassandra was known for two real predictions, made thirteen years apart, both regarding the same two people in a classic fantasy series?

6. What organization was founded in 1980 by Nobel Peace Laureate Kailash Satyarthi, to campaign for the rights of children?

7. The longitude line at 2°20'14.03" East was a long-standing rival to the Greenwich meridian as the prime meridian of the world. Under what name was it popularized in a blockbuster 2003 novel, which is set in Paris among other places?

8. What Indian Ocean archipelago comprising four islands is known for a landmark 1883 event, as well as an event of smaller proportions in 2018?

9. What elite list comprising Hilary Mantel, JG Farrell, JM Coetzee and Peter Carey, did Margaret Atwood join in 2019 with her novel *The Testaments*?

10. What fictional species dwell underground in the English countryside of AD 802,701, maintaining ancient machines and accessing the surface using a series of well-like structures?

11. Theoretical physicist Kip Thorne, who won the 2017 Nobel Physics Prize for his work on gravitational waves, served as a scientific consultant for which Academy Award-winning 2014 Hollywood film?

12. Whose New Year's statement on 1 January 1946 denied the concept of his being a living god?

13. The name of which city, founded by Rajendra Chola I to commemorate his victory over the Pala dynasty, means 'the town of the Chola who took over Ganga'?

14. For negotiating a ceasefire in which conflict did the US Secretary of State Henry Kissinger win the 1973 Nobel Peace Prize?

Set 3

1. Which is the only state road transport corporation in India which doesn't have the state's name on its own?

2. Ustad Ahmad Lahori, the architect credited with constructing the Taj Mahal, is credited with which other structure built from 1639 to 1648?

3. What connects the islands of Jan Mayen, Iceland, Azores, Saint Peter and Paul Rocks, Ascension Island, Saint Helena, Tristan da Cunha, Gough Island and Bouvet Island?

4. What date, which saw festivities in Guatemala, Mexico, Honduras and El Salvador, was believed to be the end date of a 5,126-year-long cycle in the Mesoamerican Long Count calendar and believed by many to mark the end of the world?

5. Which American inventor and writer, a recipient of the United States' National Medal of Technology and Innovation, is most well-known for his books and writings related to a future technological singularity?

6. Which popular 1994 science fiction film starred Jean-Claude Van Damme as a police officer in 1994 as well as a US federal agent in 2004, with time travel allowing the two storylines to overlap?

7. The Saudi Arabian journalist and author Jamal Khashoggi was assassinated in October 2018 in Istanbul, by agents of the Saudi government. Where did the murder take place?

8. The Delhi Sultan Muhammad bin Tughlaq shifted his capital from Delhi to which Deccan fort in 1327, before returning to Delhi in 1334?

9. And which scholar, known for his travels across the Islamic world, visited India during the reign

of Muhammad bin Tughlaq, and was appointed by the Sultan as a qadi, or judge?

10. Which Swedish physician, sword swallower and public speaker was best known for his work in translating international statistics into moving graphics?

11. About 9,000 units of this iconic car were made, before the company filed for bankruptcy in 1982. Not very well known for its power and performance, what 1985 film has kept the car alive in popular imagination?

12. Who, later famous for a key role in 20th century events, served as a war correspondent for *The Morning Post* in the Second Boer War?

13. Which 2015 novel saw pre-order records on sites like Amazon.com, on account of its unexpected discovery decades after being written, and the status of the author's only other book as an American classic?

14. Which company adopted its current name on 1 January 2001, as a result of an internal competition? The name was meant to represent its will to be a global consulting leader.

8. USA, USSR, NAM

Two sides to the Cold War which lasted almost half a century. And a third side, made up of countries that chose not to align with either of the Cold War powers. The next trio is made up of the USA, the (former) USSR and the Non-Aligned Movement.

Set 1

1. What real-life 1962 event is referenced in the main battle scene in the superhero film 'X-Men: First Class'?

2. What was the Soviet program, which put Yuri Gagarin into space and carried out a total of six crewed spaceflights, named?

3. Which strategically important city, that has been battled over more than a hundred times throughout history, and whose name means 'White city' in the local language, was the location of the first Non-Aligned Movement conference in 1961?

4. Which 'benevolent dictator' and ruler of his country for 37 years served time in a Russian work camp after being captured during World War I, participated in some events of the Russian Revolution, and led an effective resistance movement against the Nazis during World War II?

5. What term, also used to describe a safety barrier used in many theaters to protect against fire, was most popularly used in a 1945 telegram sent by British Prime Minister Winston Churchill to US President Harry Truman?

6. What word is used to describe this group of six buildings in Washington DC, which included apartments as well as office spaces, one of which, the office building at 2600 Virginia Ave NW, was in the news in the early 1970s?

7. The 1975 Spring Offensive is considered the final campaign in which war that began in 1955?

8. What terms, meaning 'restructuring' and 'openness', were in popular usage from 1986 to 1991, and are associated closely with political events of those years?

9. While Pandit Jawaharlal Nehru played a key role in the formation of the Non-Aligned Movement, who was the first Indian to serve as its chairperson?

10. Who, en route to cease-fire negotiations during the Congo Crisis, was killed in a plane crash on 18 September 1961?

11. Which World War II Soviet sniper and war hero was portrayed by Jude Law in the 2001 Hollywood film *Enemy at the Gates*?

12. And which American pilot, shot down over the Soviet Union in 1960, was portrayed by Austin Stowellin the 2015 Hollywood *Bridge of Spies*?

13. What coral reef in the Pacific Ocean, consisting of 23 islands, saw all its inhabitants relocated in 1946? It is now inhabited only by a few caretakers and occasionally visited by some scientists or divers.

14. Which city, which saw action during the 2018 FIFA World Cup, was also known for being the home of philosopher Immanuel Kant, and for a mathematical problem associated with Leonard Euler?

Set 2

1. Leaving aside nations like Yugoslavia which ceased to exist are the only two nations to end their membership of the Non-Aligned Movement?

2. What branch of the United States Armed Forces is the focus of the 2020 comedy TV series starring Steve Carell and John Malkovich?

3. Which former shipyard electrician and trade union activist, the first President of his country to be elected in a popular vote, was unable to collect his Nobel Peace Prize in person in 1983, for fear he would not be allowed to return to his country?

4. What name was given to the United States-backed campaign of political repression and state terror, which involved intelligence and political assassinations, and was formally implemented in November 1975 by several right-wing dictatorships of South America?

5. Whose decision to nationalize the Suez Canal in 1956 led to the Suez Crisis, the invasion of Egypt by Israel, Britain and France?

6. What water body, whose name roughly translates as 'Sea of Islands', once had 1000+ islands that dotted its waters? Part of its former coverage area is now a desert region.

7. Which armed conflict saw NATO conduct its first military intervention after the end of the Cold War in 1991?

8. Which three countries, formerly part of the Soviet Union, joined NATO in 2004, the only former Soviet states to do so?

9. An anti-government uprising in which country on 28 February 1947 led to the White Terror, a period of 38 years of martial law which saw brutal suppression of political dissidents?

10. Which country's communist revolution serves as the backdrop for a significant portion of the iconic crime film *The Godfather Part II*?

11. Which countries, part of a Cold War conflict zone, remain officially at war due to the absence of a formal peace treaty ending the conflict?

12. Which former capital of a European country continues to hold an unofficial status as a second capital, and served as the seat of government for 9 years after the capital was moved to its present location?

13. While the term non-alignment was first used in 1953, and the Non-Aligned Movement itself was formed in 1961, in which year was the term 'Non-Aligned Movement' first used to refer to its participant countries?

14. For what reason did Colombia and Peru suspend their participation in the Non-Alignment movement in 2019?

Set 3

1. Which Indian revolutionary, wanted in colonial India for his attempt to smuggle in German arms, fled via Japan and China to the United States and then Mexico, where he was introduced to Marxism, leading him to meet Lenin in 1920, and making him a key player in the Soviet plans to introduce Marxism in India? He was eventually to withdraw from politics and focus on 'radical humanism'.

2. In his first appearance, who was sent on an assignment from Brussels to the Soviet Union to report on the policies of Stalin's Bolshevik government?

3. Which James Bond novel by Ian Fleming is partly set on the iconic *Orient Express* passenger train?

4. Located in the Friedrichstadt neighborhood, it is believed to derive its name on account of it being the third such location set up by the Allies. On the opposite side, it was simply called the *Border*

Crossing Point. What am I talking about, now a tourist attraction?

5. Which President of his country, known for human rights abuses during his tenure, started off with support from Israel and the Western powers, until his decision to nationalize industries in 1972 and turn towards the Soviet Union for support?

6. Which book begins with the lines "A spectre is haunting Europe—the spectre of communism. All the powers of old Europe have entered into a holy alliance to exorcise this spectre"?

7. Which country saw mass killings of over 500,000 people in violent anti-communist purges, following an aborted coup on 01 October 1965, for which the country's Communist Party was blamed?

8. The former British territories of the Gold Coast, Ashanti, the Northern Territories and British Togoland were unified into which single independent country, on 6 March 1957?

9. Which country was extensively bombed from 1964-1973 to both deter the country's communist forces fighting against the royalist government, and to prevent communist forces in the neighboring country from using it as a base?

10. Who served variously as the King and Prime Minister of Cambodia, including serving as a figurehead head of state under the Khmer Rouge for a year?

11. What reason led to the invasion and holding of 52 American diplomats as hostages, for a period of 444 days, by Iranian revolutionaries?

12. The Iran-Iraq war was notable for some countries like the United States, Soviet Union and Yugoslavia providing both sides with arms. Which country provided Iraq with almost $8 billion in financial support, little aware of how it would soon be paid back?

13. In the 1989 season of Revolutions, which European country saw the only violent overthrow of its communist government, along with the execution of its President?

14. Which country saw more than 300,000 Cuban forces support the pro-Communist forces against US & South Africa backed independence movements?

9. DC, MARVEL, AND EVERYONE ELSE

In the world of comics (and now cinema), there has always been DC Comics and Marvel Comics. And I categorized everyone else into a Third Front to close the trio and ensure we have some collective competition to the big two.

Set 1

1. Which comic book series was recognized in *Time*'s *List of the 100 Best Novels* as one of the best English language novels published since 1923?

2. Who moves to Mumbai on a scholarship with his aunt Maya and uncle Bhim, carries on a romance with Meera Jain, a girl from his school, and is given the powers of a spider by an ancient yogi to fight evil in the world?

3. Which town is depicted as medium-sized, and as having beaches, lakes, rivers, deserts, farmland, woods, mountains, a transit system and four distinct seasons? Most of the residents we know attend the 11th grade.

4. What fictional US state gets its name from a blend of two real US states, supposedly to allow all kinds of weather or climate in the stories? We know it as the location of Duckburg.

5. Fill in the blanks in this list: Adam West, Michael Keaton, Val Kilmer, _____ _____, Christian Bale, Ben Affleck, Robert Pattinson.

6. How do we better Otto Octavius, a nuclear physicist whose radiation-resistant apparatus fused with his body following an explosion?

7. What historical relic plays a central role in the Keanu Reeves starrer *Constantine*, based on the *Hellblazer* comic book series?

8. Which extremely popular Marvel Cinematic Universe character is based on a character after whom a day of the week is named?

9. Chris Evans is very well known for portraying Captain America in the Marvel Cinematic Universe films. But which other Marvel Comics character has he portrayed on film?

10. The critically and commercially successful film *The Dark Knight* famously won Heath Ledger a posthumous Best Supporting Actor Oscar at the Academy Awards. Which category did it win its only other Oscar in?

11. What aptly named character, a companion of the series protagonist, was a former witch cursed by the Witch's Council to spend 100 years as a cat, as punishment for trying to take over the world?

12. In the 2018 film *Deadpool 2*, Deadpool famously uses a time tracking device to go back in time and kill Ryan Reynolds (the actor playing Deadpool) before the latter does what?

13. Which Harvey Comics character debuted in 1953 and has been portrayed on screen by Macaulay Culkin in a 1994 film? He is typically shown wearing a waistcoat, a white shirt with a giant red bow tie, and blue shorts.

14. The iconic graphic novel *Maus* is known for its portrayal of people from different countries as animals. Jews are chosen as mice, Germans as cats, Poles as pigs and Swedes as reindeer. What are the Americans and French shown as?

Set 2

1. What connects Lee Meriwether, Michelle Pfeiffer, Halle Berry and Anne Hathaway, with Zoe Kravitz set to join the list as of 2020?

2. In 2014, it became the first soundtrack album consisting entirely of previously released songs to top the *Billboard 200* charts. Which movie is this album from, in which the protagonist listens to the songs on a mixtape using his Walkman?

3. Which fictional character, the son of a boxer, is a graduate from Columbia Law School and operates out of the Hell's Kitchen neighborhood in New York City?

4. What 1998 comic book series about a famous event in 480 BC was inspired by a 1962 film the writer saw as a young boy, and in turn, led to a commercially successful 2006 film adaptation?

5. What iconic comic book series features individual stories called 'yarns', in an American West town

with an incredibly high crime rate, and controlled by the Roark family, a dynasty of corrupt landowners and politicians?

6. In the graphic novel *The Sandman: The Wake*, Superman, Batman, and the Martian Manhunter are seen discussing their dreams. Superman and Batman mention the dreams they have, but Martian Manhunter claims he never had such dreams. What are they talking about?

7. This antagonist seeks to control space and time to bring balance to the universe. What fitting name does he have, a short form of a Greek name meaning 'immortal'?

8. Wesley Dodds was the first DC Comics fictional character to bear this name. Attired in a green business suit, fedora, and gas mask, he uses a gun emitting a sleeping gas to sedate criminals. He later uses sand and a blowtorch that he could use to quickly create walls. What character is this?

9. Which actor, famous for his role in another film franchise, is known among DC Comics fans for voicing the supervillain Joker in animated films and video games for over two decades?

10. Some sources place it north of Tanzania, in the area that is Burundi. Others show it between South Sudan, Uganda, Kenya and Ethiopia. Some aspects have also been inspired by the Kingdom of Lesotho. What fictional nation am I talking about?

11. What historic 1973 event in Europe features in the 2014 superhero film *X-Men: Days of Future Past*?

12. Which comic book series features characters such as Campion Bond (the grandfather of James Bond), as well as creations of authors such as HG Wells, Bram Stoker and Jules Verne?

13. *Ramayana 3392 AD* is a re-imagining of the historical classic *Ramayana* in a post-apocalyptic future. While the original has the antagonist Ravana capable of shapeshifting thanks to a divine boon, what enables him to shapeshift in the post-apocalyptic version?

14. Stephen Strange was an egotistical doctor before damaging his hands in a car crash. He eventually becomes the Marvel superhero Doctor Strange. But, what kind of doctor was he before the crash?

Set 3

1. What fictional island, which features in the works of Plato, is also the home of a popular DC Comics superhero?

2. What connects the heroic spacefarer Spaceman Spiff, the private eye Tracer Bullet and the masked superhero Stupendous Man?

3. Which Marvel Comics superhero played a key role (or should I say roles) in the 2018 film which won the *Best Animated Feature Film* award that year?

4. What graphic novel written by Max Allan Collins was adapted into a 2002 crime drama film starring Tom Hanks, Paul Newman and Jude Law?

5. The character's original name was borrowed from the nickname of the creator's first girlfriend. In English translations, a specific name was chosen because of the dog's color, and because it fit the speech balloons, on account of having the same number of letters as the original. Give me the English name. For bonus points, the original name as well.

6. The original French for fixation or obsession is also a pun of which character's name in the Asterix comics?

7. The plot of which graphic novel written by Alan Moore begins on 05 November 1997 in London?

8. What superhero group featured members like Robin, Speedy, Lilith, Bumblebee, Kid Flash and Aqualad?

9. Which legendary actor portrayed Jor-El in the first *Superman* film, earning $3.7 million for just 10 minutes of screen time?

10. Barrier Lake is a man-made reservoir created for hydroelectric power generation in Alberta, Canada. What iconic location was it used to portray in a 2003 film based on Marvel Comics characters?

11. What was the original name of the superhero, a boy who, by speaking a magic word, could

transform into a costumed adult with superpowers?

12. How do we better know the rainbow bridge which extends from Earth to the realm of the gods, being guarded at the latter point by the god Heimdall?

13. Albert Simmons, a trained assassin, is himself murdered and goes to Hell. What does he come back as, after making a deal with the devil, setting the stage for the comic books series named after him?

14. What comic book series written by Mark Millar and Dave Gibbons was originally known as *The Secret Service* before being branded following a successful 2014 film adaptation?

10. BRITISH, PORTUGUESE AND OTHER FOREIGN RULERS IN INDIA

We all know the British ruled and exploited most of India for 190 years. The Portuguese were around for 451 years. The other European powers controlled large parts of land for significant portions of time, but eventually faded, save for the French. And that's the next trio – British, Portuguese and other rulers in India.

Set 1

1. What 14x18 feet structure gained notoriety for events on the night of 20 June 1756? It was later used as a warehouse. A memorial to the events was built and now stands in St. John's Church, Kolkata.

2. This Frenchman served as personal physician to the Mughal prince Dara Shikoh and was later attached to the court of Emperor Aurangzeb for 12 years. He is most well-known for his 1684 publication which is considered the first published classification of humans into distinct races. Name him.

3. After what event on 25 April 1974 did the Portuguese government recognize the legality of

Indian sovereignty in Goa, more than 12 years after the former Portuguese colony was annexed by India?

4. The male Aldabra giant tortoise *Adwaita*, who died at the age of 255 in the Alipore Zoological Gardens of Kolkata in 2006, originally lived on whose estate in the Northern Kolkata suburbs?

5. Which former French territory overwhelmingly voted, through a 1948 plebiscite, to become part of India? The French government ceded control in 1951, and the territory was integrated into the state of West Bengal in 1954.

6. Which privateer serving the Vijayanagara Empire convinced Afonso de Albuquerque to conquer Goa in 1510?

7. Goa was ruled by the Portuguese from 1510 to 1961. But for a brief period from 1799 to 1813, during the Napoleonic Wars, which foreign power occupied Goa?

8. The port of Surat was ruled by the Mughals in the 17th century, with trading posts established by the Dutch and British. Whose 1664 raid on the city significantly reduced trade in the city?

9. Which town in the Indian state of Bihar, also known as mini Kashi, was the scene of a key British East India Company victory in 1764?

10. Under which treaty did the British East India Company cede Kashmir to Gulab Singh, the Raja of Jammu, for 7.5 million rupees, in 1846?

11. Which Frenchman, who figures prominently in the novels of Alexandre Dumas, is considered as one of the prime movers behind the setting up of the French East India Company?

12. Another 1954 liberation. Which Portuguese territory was freed from colonial rule by local volunteer groups on 11 August 1954?

13. During the British Raj, Indian princely states were granted gun salutes based on their size and importance. Which five princely states received the highest recognition, with a 21 gun salute?

14. Which fort, located near the present-day of Cuddalore and lying in ruins, was sold by the Marathas to the highest European bidder, with the British winning it and taking it over in 1690? It briefly served as the British headquarters in Southern India and passed hands between the French and British a few times before finally falling into British possession in 1785.

Set 2

1. Which is the first (and as of 2019, the only) state in India to have a uniform civil code in place, allowing the same laws to apply to all citizens regardless of their religion?

2. India's first adhesive stamp, the Scinde Dawk, was introduced in 1852 by Sir Bartle Frere. How did it get its name?

3. The Indian Union Territory of Pondicherry is made up of four former territories of French

India, comprising the main Pondicherry district, Mahe, Karaikal and Yanam. Which of these was the last to be occupied by France?

4. Which prominent Indian independence activist called for Direct Action against Portuguese rule, in a speech in Goa on 18 June 1946?

5. What land revenue system was introduced in 1820 by Thomas Munro, which allowed the government to deal directly with cultivators for revenue collection?

6. The town of Tharangambadi was originally established in 1620 as the first trading post of which European country in India?

7. Which 1969 film about a group of Indians attempting to liberate Goa from Portuguese rule featured superstar Amitabh Bachchan in his first acting role?

8. The Goa National Congress was founded in 1928 by which Goan activist, who is known as the father of Goan Nationalism?

9. Which Indian city is now named after Archibald _____, a naval surveyor who voyaged to the region in 1788, and originally named the city after Lord Cornwallis?

10. The 1849 Last Treaty of Lahore between Duleep Singh and the East India Company led to the surrender of what item to the Queen of England?

11. Which town, described as a post since 300 BCE, was a Portuguese trading post from 1502 until

1609 when it was occupied by the Dutch, who used it extensively for transporting slaves?

12. The islands of Bombay famously came to the British as part of the dowry of the Portuguese princess Catherine of Braganza, when she married Charles II of England. England then leased the islands to the English East India Company for what sum in 1668?

13. The Enfield Pattern 1853 rifle-musket, introduced in 1856, was a key contributor to the 1857 Indian war of independence, due to rumors that its cartridges, which had to be bitten to tear open, were greased with animal fat. Which company made these rifles?

14. Which colonial power did not set up colonies in India, thus adhering to the Treaty of Tordesillas it signed in 1494 with Portugal, dividing the newly discovered lands among the two powers?

Set 3

1. Which city, for some time the capital of Portuguese India, hosted the grave of Vasco da Gama until his remains were returned to Portugal in 1539?

2. The British Raj set up the first High Courts in India in 1862, in the three Presidencies in Calcutta, Bombay and Madras. In which city was the fourth High Court set up in 1866?

3. Which Indian ruler is known to have sent emissaries and diplomatic missions to the

Ottoman Empire, the Durrani Empire, and France, to form alliances against the East India Company?

4. The Commonwealth Games are played among athletes from the British Commonwealth. What Games are played by countries having a history with Portugal?

5. The British organized the Delhi Durbar three times, in 1877, 1903 and 1911, to mark the succession of an Emperor or Empress of India. On which of these occasions was the sovereign already a ruler of Great Britain? And who?

6. The Xendi tax was a discriminatory religious tax imposed on Hindus in Portuguese Goa in the 17th century. What does Xendi mean?

7. One of the world's largest cannons at the time, the Thanjavur cannon weighing over 22 tonnes was cast in 1620. Which European country's technical knowhow was supposedly used to cast the cannon for the Thanjavur Nayaka dynasty?

8. Which present-day metropolis did the French Governor-General of India Joseph Dupleix succeed in capturing from the British in 1746?

9. The Basilica of Bom Jesus in Old Goa holds the mortal remains of which Catholic saint, whose Feast is observed on 3 December every year?

10. And which church located in Panaji, Goa was first built in 1541 and has its festival every year on 8 December?

11. What did Netaji Subhas Chandra Bose rename as 'Shaheed' and 'Swaraj' (meaning 'martyr' and 'self-rule' respectively) in 1943, during his only visit to the region?

12. What word, meaning "Land of the pure", was coined by Choudhry Rahmat Ali in his 1933 pamphlet *Now or Never?*

13. Which country, originally part of British India, became a separately administered colony of Britain in 1937, eventually becoming independent in 1948?

14. Which former Viceroy of India played a key role in the policy of appeasement of Adolf Hitler from 1936-38, and later served as British Ambassador to the United States?

11. BRAIN, BRAWN, BEAUTY

No, this is not something I came up with while watching Survivor. Literature has always shown this trio as black and white – Beauty and the Beast, Mind vs. Brawn and so on. But they fit quite nicely into a set of three.

Set 1

1. Where did the highly publicized 1972 World Chess Championship between Boris Spassky of the Soviet Union and Bobby Fischer of the United States take place?

2. The United States is the clear leader in the all-time medals tally at the Summer Olympics. As of 2020, which country led the all-time tally at the Winter Olympics?

3. The Gothic architectural innovation of replacing thick walls with rib vaults and buttresses, and using stained glass to fill the openings, came about due to what spiritual need?

4. At what iconic venue did the reigning chess champion Garry Kasparov defeat the challenger, Viswanathan Anand, by a margin of 10.5 to 7.5, in the Classical World Chess Championship 1995?

5. India won the field hockey gold medal at all the Summer Olympics Games from 1928 to 1964, save for Rome 1960 when it had to settle for silver. Who beat India 1-0 in the final to win the gold that year?

6. What connects Reita Faria, Aishwarya Rai, Diana Hayden, Yukta Mookhey, Priyanka Chopra and Manushi Chillar? More ladies may join this list in the future.

7. Which Indian teacher, philosopher and economist features prominently in the Buddhist text *Mahavamsa* as well as the Sanskrit play *Mudrarakshasa* by Vishakhadatta?

8. Which former Mr. Universe and Mr. Olympia now has a professional bodybuilding and strongman event named after him? The event is held annually in Columbus in the United States. We know him better for his work in other fields.

9. Which former Miss Universe contestant and fitness instructor for her country's defense forces made her film debut in the action film *Fast & Furious*?

10. Which Indian, the 1976 rediscovery of whose 'lost notebook' of work from the last year of his life led to a lot of excitement in mathematical circles, was the first Indian to be elected a Fellow of Trinity College, Cambridge?

11. Which Australian cricketer and winner of two ODI World Cup titles, was also known for hurling a haggis a distance of 230 feet in 1989?

12. Which cosmetic product, introduced to the Indian market by Hindustan Unilever in 1975, was rebranded in 2020 due to criticism for promoting colorism? What was it renamed as?

13. Who has been described by the University Central Hospital in Helsinki, Finland as lacking the 17 to 22 percent body fat required for a woman to menstruate? Her bathroom scale from 1965 was permanently set at 110 pounds, which is 35 pounds underweight for a woman of her height.

14. Who is around 50 feet tall, wears only a pair of briefs, earrings, and gumboots, has exceptional physical strength, and came from the planet Jupiter but stayed on Earth after tasting parathas and halwa?

Set 2

1. The CrossFit Games are an annual athletic competition and have been held every year since 2007. What controversial item did the 2016 Games winners receive, leading to backlash from many, including some winners as well?

2. How do we know the 22-year old Mexican American woman from Queens, New York, who is sorely lacking in fashion sense, wears braces, and works at a high fashion magazine based in Manhattan?

3. The author adopted this name in 1718, though he was known to have used over a hundred pen

names during his lifetime. It is an anagram of the Latinized spelling of his surname and the initial letters of *le jeune* "the young". The name also conveys connotations of speed and daring. Which Enlightenment era writer and philosopher am I talking about?

4. How do we better know Ghulam Mohammad Baksh Butt, who was born in Amritsar, India, and remained undefeated in a 52-year long wrestling career?

5. Which science fiction and detective fiction writer, a recipient of an honorary doctorate from Oxford University, was also a publisher, illustrator, and calligrapher, but was most well-known for his work in films?

6. Who, in 2014, became the first person of Indian descent to win the *Miss America* competition?

7. And what event began in 1968 to protest the lack of diversity in the *Miss America* competition?

8. Which Italian scientist and polymath, considered by many as the 'father of modern science', is mentioned multiple times in a song by the band Queen?

9. Which Persian polymath, known to have authored over 450 works (of which 240 have survived) was most well-known for his books on medicine, including *The Canon of Medicine*, a medical encyclopedia that became a standard text at many medieval universities?

10. Which chess prodigy, known for winning a game without looking at the board at age 5, was the first woman to surpass the 2700-Elo rating in chess?

11. The first Indian sportsman to be nominated to the Rajya Sabha (upper house) of Parliament, which professional wrestler was best known for his on-screen portrayal of Hanuman?

12. What traditional sport from the Indian subcontinent features a gymnast performing yoga postures and wrestling grips using a vertical pole, cane, or rope?

13. What traditional event, typically practiced in the Indian state of Tamil Nadu, features a bull released into a crowd of people, with multiple human participants attempting to grab the hump on the bull's back and hanging on to it while the bull attempts to escape?

14. What controversial item, now common especially in Western society, was banned in many countries following its launch in 1946? A 1951 contest featuring it even led to Pope Pius XII condemning the winner.

Set 3

1. The 1996 edition of Miss World, held in Bangalore, India, was organized by whose entertainment company?

2. Who is the only person in history to have won a Nobel Prize, an Academy Award, and a Grammy Award?

3. Which prolific inventor and engineer, an early proponent of wireless communication, spent his last few years in obscurity, and was forgotten after his death in 1943 until an SI unit was named in his honor in 1960?

4. The year 1642 saw the death of a prominent engineer and scientist in January. December of the same year saw the birth of another mathematician and scientist. The former is known for his discovery of several celestial bodies, while the latter is known for formulating laws explaining the behavior of such bodies. Name both.

5. Older manuscripts like the Dead Sea Scrolls refer to his height as 'four cubits and a span', or 6 feet 9 inches, while later sources say his height was 9 feet 9 inches. Who are we talking about? The name is frequently used to describe the stronger party in underdog stories.

6. After which mathematical prodigy is the triangular tabular representation of binomial coefficients commonly named, even though it was studied before him in ancient India, where it was called Meru-prastaara, and ancient Persia, where it was named after Khayyam?

7. When Michael Phelps won his eighth gold medal at the 2008 Beijing Games, whose 1972 record of seven first-place finishes at a single Olympic Games did he break?

8. Her name is considered by some scholars to mean 'risen from foam', referring to her creation from foam created by Uranus's genitals which his son Cronos severed & threw into the sea?

9. Which ancient Indian physician is considered the 'father of plastic surgery'?

10. One of the more memorable characters from the Game of Thrones series, who stands eight feet tall and is known for his extremely cruel nature, uncontrollable temper, and prowess in battle?

11. What rating system, used to calculate relative skill levels of players in zero-sum games such as chess, is named after its Hungarian-American creator?

12. Which ancient philosopher's main body of work is compiled into four sections – units of time, mensuration, methods for determining the positions of planets, and trigonometric aspects of the celestial sphere?

13. How do we better know Dame Lesley Lawson, a prominent teenage model during the sixties, who was known for her thin build and androgynous appearance?

14. What 1975 sports event, held at the Araneta Coliseum, was named after one of the participants boasted that the event would be "a killa and a _____ and a chilla, when I get that gorilla in _____".

12. CREATE, PRESERVE, DESTROY

Brahma, Vishnu and Shiva – the holy trinity of Hinduism. They also symbolize aspects of the universe – Brahma is the Creator of all existence, Vishnu the Preserver, and Shiva the Destroyer. And this forms our next trio.

Set 1

1. The author of this seminal work, in his own words, noted that he began work on the topic in 1837, drew up some notes in 1844, and continued working on the subject until its publication on 24 November 1859. The book became very popular as it was written for non-scientific readers, and is now considered the foundation of evolutionary biology. Name the book and its author.

2. Which scholar and researcher, known as *Tamil Thatha* (the Grandfather of Tamil), collected over 3,000 paper and palm-leaf manuscripts over five decades, thus bringing many long-forgotten works of classical Tamil literature to light?

3. Which avatar of the Hindu deity Vishnu is known for saving Manu and the seven sages from a giant deluge, and rescuing the holy Vedas from a demon called Hayagriva?

4. Which mythological event, foretold to lead to the death of a number of great figures and the submersion of the world in water, leading to a new and renewed world, is referred to as 'Fate of the Gods' in the ancient tongue of the country? You probably know it for sharing a name with a blockbuster superhero movie.

5. What institution, termed the nation's attic for its holdings of 150 million items, 21 libraries, 9 research centers, zoo and 19 museums, was founded in 1846 for the 'increase and diffusion of knowledge'?

6. Wh god is depicted with four hands, with one hand holding the sacred texts, the second holding rosary beads symbolizing time, the third holding a ladle like instrument symbolizing the means to feed the sacrificial fire, and the fourth a utensil with water symbolizing the means where all creation emanates from?

7. In the Genesis creation narrative, God creates heaven and earth in six days and rests on the seventh. On which day does he create man?

8. The demon Narakasura's killing by Krishna, the eighth avatar of Lord Vishnu, is celebrated the night before the festival of Diwali in many cultures. He is considered in some legends as the son of Bhumidevi (Earth) and who?

9. What state of liberation from repeated rebirth, a common theme in Eastern religions, is also the name of a grunge music band?

10. Which M. Night Shyamalan film features plant life developing a defense mechanism against humans, in the form of an airborne toxin that forces humans to kill themselves?

11. This act is believed to happen due to the actions of deities seeking divine retribution. Historic arguments suggest that sudden changes in sea levels after the last glacial period 8,000 years ago could have inspired myths about these events. What event/myth is this, which is a common theme in many religions across the world?

12. Whose predictions, focused on Earth at the center of the universe, served for 1500 years as the basis for all astronomical charts until Copernicus published his heliocentric model in 1543?

13. What critically acclaimed film is set on a future inhabitable Earth, focusing on a trash compactor robot whose goal is to pick up garbage?

14. In Douglas Adams' science fiction series *The Hitchhiker's Guide to the Galaxy*, the character Slartibartfast is a planet designer. For designing what geographical feature on Earth does he win an award?

Set 2

1. Which Hindu god of war is variously named *Saravanabhava* (born among the reeds), *Dandapani* (wielder of the mace) and *Sanmukha* (six faced)? He is also the subject of the epic poem

Kumarasambhava by Kalidasa. No single answer here, but one of his popular names will do.

2. Which capital city was founded in 1325, based on a prophecy that said that wandering tribes should build their city at a location signalled by an eagle with a snake in its beak atop a cactus? Also name the new city built on top of its ruins after its capture in 1521.

3. What term was first used in a 1949 BBC broadcast by Fred Hoyle, who favored an alternate 'steady state' model but used the term to describe Georges Lemaitre's 'primeval atom' model?

4. The only area in Asia where a particular species still survives, it was set up in the late 19th century by the local ruler when British colonial officials pointed out the species decline to him. The ruler eventually fled to Pakistan, but the sanctuary continues to this date in India as a national park. What region and which species am I talking about?

5. What landmark film, the most expensive of its time, was the first black and white film in India to be digitally colored and released in 2004? Both the original and the re-release were commercial successes.

6. Who famously quoted from the Bhagavad Gita "Now I am become Death, the destroyer of worlds" on 16 July 1945?

7. Give me a one-word term for the part of the eukaryotic cell cycle in which replicated

chromosomes are separated into two new nuclei. Cell division gives rise to genetically identical cells in which the total number of chromosomes is maintained.

8. Which hero in ancient Mesopotamian mythology undergoes a series of trials hoping to attain immortality, but eventually fails the trials and returns home realizing that immortality is beyond his reach?

9. Which national park was created when US President Abraham Lincoln signed a bill protecting the area in 1864? This was the first instance of parkland being set aside specifically for preservation and public use by the action of the U.S. federal government.

10. What composition, unfinished at the time of its creator's death, was later completed by several of the creator's contemporaries? One of the stories surrounding the composition is that the creator believed he was writing it for his own funeral.

11. In Greek mythology, who was the first human woman created by Hephaestus on the instructions of Zeus? Each god is believed to have given her gifts, though she is remembered better for an item she carried with her.

12. Which key figure behind the Bombay Natural History Society and pioneer of his field, first got into the field at the age of 34? The venture was courtesy of his inability to find a suitable job, leading to a move to Kihim, a coastal village near

Mumbai, where he got a chance to study the baya weaver from close quarters?

13. What 1998 film featured a comet called Wolf-Beidermanset to collide with Earth and cause a mass extinction?

14. What process, considered an important step to living well in the afterlife, featured elaborate rituals such as dehydration using natron for 70 days, and cleansing of the abdominal cavity using palm wine and spices?

Set 3

1. The United States Declaration of Independence, made on July 4, 1776, was signed by representatives from thirteen states, which in turn became the first thirteen states of the independent USA. What state, formerly a part of one of the original thirteen, became the fourteenth state in 1791?

2. Which city, sacked twice by Persia, given the status of a free city under Roman rule, and which spent over 300 years under Ottoman rule, has been inhabited for over 500 years, and is known both for its classical civilization as well as its significance in the world of sports?

3. In which year did the Parliament of India enact the first comprehensive Wildlife Protection Act to protect plant and animal species in India?

4. What term, which in Abrahamic religions refers to a time of the second coming of the Messiah,

the resurrection of the righteous and the coming of Judgment Day, is also the name of a 1999 Arnold Schwarzenegger movie?

5. This word was first recorded in 1819 to refer to an Afro-Brazilian rebel leader. The word is commonly used in Haitian folklore and has been associated with voodoo. The modern interpretation of the word came about from fans of a 1968 movie by George Romero. What word, which has sparked a genre of its own in the world of entertainment?

6. Which Indian region is believed to have been created by recovering land from the sea? Sangam legends attribute this to the Chera king Senguttuvan who threw his spear into the sea, while other works credit an avatar of Vishnu who threw his axe into the sea.

7. Which Hindu religious sect, known for its sustainable living methods, follows a set of twenty-nine principles given by their founder Guru Jambeshwar? Eight of the twenty-nine principles focus on preserving biodiversity.

8. Who is the Greek goddess who enacts retribution against those who commit arrogance before the gods? The word has been used by both Isaac Asimov and Agatha Christie to name their novels.

9. Which twin brothers, believed to be born of a vestal virgin Rhea Silvia and the god Mars, are believed to have been suckled by a she-wolf in their infancy?

10. What non-violent movement, believed to have begun in 1973 in Uttarakhand, India, has played a key role in tree conservation in India? Participants, mostly women, started it off by hugging trees to prevent their being cut down.

11. What 6th century pair of statues, hewn from sandstone cliffs and then finished using mud mixed with straw, stood 35 and 53 meters tall until their destruction in 2001 by the Taliban?

12. Which region, also known as Dardania, unilaterally declared its independence from Serbia in 2008?

13. Which animal, now found in the wild primarily in Africa, was once abundant in India, until being hunted out? The last three individuals in the wild are believed to have been killed by Maharaj Ramanuj Pratap Singh of Surgujain 1947?

14. What fictional neural network-based artificial super-intelligence was created by Cyberdyne Systems, and destroyed most of mankind in a nuclear attack after it gained self-awareness and humans tried to deactivate it?

13. RED, GREEN, BLUE

Different colors have been called primary colors over time, but thanks to the high proportion of my adult life spent in front of a computer screen, I consider Red, Green and Blue, or RGB in short, as the three primary colors. And this forms my next trio.

Set 1

1. What bird, also called the redbird, has a distinctive crest on the head and a mask on the face, the latter being black in the male and grey in the female? It is also the state bird of seven US states, more than any other.

2. From 1969 to 2011, which was the only country in the world to have a flag with only a single color (green), and with no design, insignia, or other details on it at all?

3. What bright color, #007FFF on the hexadecimal scale, and described as the color of the sky on a clear day, takes its name from a semi-precious stone, and is used to refer to the part of a Mediterranean coastline as well as a cloud computing platform?

4. Which river, dyed green every year in observance of St. Patrick's Day, had its flow reversed using man-made locks and canals, to reduce the risk of

extreme weather events, as well as improve sanitation and transport?

5. What color, derived from the French word for chestnut, is also the color of robes worn by Vajrayana Buddhist monks, the state color of Queensland, and features in the name of a pop-rock band formerly called *Kara's Flowers*?

6. The semi-precious stone from question 3 above. It was mined as early as the 7th millennium BC in northeast Afghanistan, was highly valued by the Indus Valley civilization, and was used in the funeral mask of Tutankhamen. It was also ground into powder and used in blue Renaissance paintings in medieval Europe. What stone is this?

7. Which mosque constructed between 1609 and 1616, was built with six minarets? When the Sultan was told that the mosque in Mecca had six minarets, and thus the new mosque should not have six, he ordered a seventh minaret to be added to the mosque in Mecca. The mosque still functions and is known as the Blue Mosque for the hand-painted blue tiles that adorn it.

8. Verdigris is the common name for a green pigment formed when copper is exposed to air or seawater over time. Which famous 151-foot-tall statue, originally a copper color, turned green around 1900 and has stayed that way ever since?

9. What now commonplace item was first seen in 1868 outside the Houses of Parliament in London, grew in popularity in the early 20th

century on both sides of the Atlantic, and soon evolved into its modern avatar having (with some minor variations) three colors of red, green and amber?

10. Which famous post-Impressionist painting shows the view from the painter's asylum room, and used ultramarine and cobalt blue for the sky, and Indian yellow and zinc yellow for the stars?

11. What supernatural creature, depicted as a little bearded man wearing a green coat and hat, is known for engaging in mischief and is believed by many to have a pot of gold hidden at the end of the rainbow?

12. What color gets its name from a popular type and region of wine? The name is also a region in France and the name of multiple former kingdoms in Europe.

13. What English term is synonymous with 'becoming very angry' and 'losing one's patience'?

14. What is responsible for the red color on Mars' surface, leading to it being called the Red Planet?

Set 2

1. What term is used to describe a late phase of stellar evolution that has exhausted the supply of hydrogen in its core and begun the thermonuclear fusion of hydrogen in a shell surrounding the core? Such a star will be tens to hundreds of times larger than our Sun, but with a lower outer temperature, giving it its distinctive color.

2. The period is believed to have lasted from the spring of 1901 to 1904. It is defined by mostly monochromatic paintings in a particular shade. The somberness of the color and the depressing subject matter is attributed to the creator's journey through Spain and to the suicide of a friend, leading him to be severely depressed. What are we talking about?

3. Which American singer-songwriter and guitarist, nicknamed 'The King of the Blues', grew up on a cotton plantation in Mississippi, was attracted to music and the guitar in church, and began his career in local joints and radio?

4. What alcoholic beverage, often portrayed as a dangerously addictive hallucinogen, has been commonly referred to in literature as "the green fairy"?

5. Located in the center of the land, what lies at the end of the yellow brick road, and is centered around the Royal Palace? All visitors are asked to wear green-tinted spectacles to protect their eyes from the 'brightness and glory' of the city.

6. The term derives from poker, where the highest value came to be associated with a certain color. It is believed to have been first used in a stock market in the 1920s, by Oliver Gingold, an early employee of the company that would become Dow Jones. What is the term, synonymous with a reputation for quality and reliability?

7. Which country's flag is blue and white, with a white cross on an azure background in the top left, and nine alternating blue and white stripes? The stripes are traditionally believed to represent the nine syllables of the phrase "Freedom or Death" in the country's language.

8. This sport evolved out of earlier outdoor lawn-based sports, and this is reflected in the typically green cloth called baize that covers the 'playing area'. What sport am I talking about?

9. The veins carrying fluids in and out get gradually closed off, and water and mineral intake is reduced. Over time, chlorophyll content goes down and xanthophyll and beta-carotene content is revealed. What phenomenon is this, which occurs once a year?

10. What term, used in literary fiction to lead readers towards a wrong conclusion, was popularized in 1807 by William Cobbett, who told a story of using a strong-smelling smoked fish to divert and distract hounds from chasing a rabbit?

11. The presence of what gas in the upper atmosphere of Uranus gives the planet its distinctive blue-green color?

12. What apparel company was started in San Francisco in 1873, after receiving a patent for a particular design? They started manufacturing their signature product only in the 1870s, contrary to public belief that it was first made to

cater to miners in the California Gold Rush, which peaked in 1849.

13. For which movie was Scarlett Johansson nominated for a *Best Supporting Actress* Academy Award, for her role as the secret anti-Nazi Rosie?

14. Which organization's members are known for their characteristic white saris with three blue borders? The blue borders signify the vows members take, of poverty, obedience, and chastity and wholehearted service to the poorest of the poor.

Set 3

1. The presence of what metal in emeralds (a variety of beryl) provides them with their characteristic green color?

2. What term is used to describe, in 19th century maritime folklore, an afterlife for sailors who had served at least fifty years at sea? The term appears in literature as well, including in a novella by Herman Melville. In Neil Gaiman's *The Sandman* comic book series, it is shown as a place in the Dreaming.

3. Due to the immense popularity of a 1930s Coca Cola campaign, an urban legend was spawned that he wears red and white because they are the colors of Coca Cola. However, he had been shown in red and white clothes earlier as well – in ads for White Rock Beverages in 1915 and 1923,

and on several covers of *Puck* magazine. Who am I talking about?

4. What name is given to Lord Shiva for his act of consuming the Halahal poison from the ocean of milk? The potent poison changed his neck to a blue color.

5. Which country's official residence of the head of state, built in the country's traditional architectural style and with grounds spanning 62 acres, is informally called the 'Blue House'?

6. Which people, traditionally nomadic pastoralists, have been called the 'blue people' for the indigo dye colored clothes they traditionally wear and which stains their skin?

7. Which country's flag, considered one of the oldest national symbols and first recorded in 1230, is believed to have been designed by Duke Leopold V after the Siege of Acre. The duke's surcoat was drenched in blood during the battle, but when he removed his belt, the cloth underneath was still white and unstained, creating a white band.

8. What popular green colored dip, first developed in Mexico, has become a staple of American cuisine, especially on Super Bowl Sunday and Cinco de Mayo?

9. The primary antagonist of which crime TV show, a serial killer with a vast network of operatives who killed over 70 people, and who founded and

led a secret organization called the Blake Association, was called Red John?

10. Which king's murder, as revenge for breaking a marriage agreement, is depicted in the *Red Wedding* scene in the *Game of Thrones* franchise?

11. Ochre is a natural clay earth pigment ranging in color from yellow to deep orange to brown. What component of ochre, when present in large quantities, imparts it a reddish tint known as 'red ochre'?

12. What do you get when *Camellia sinensis* leaves and buds are not subject to oxidation and withering, both processes being followed for more popular variants?

13. The 'Buddha for Universal Peace', a 2.7-meter high statue, was modeled on the Buddha statue in Bodh Gaya, and is touring the world to raise awareness of Buddhism and promote peace. Of what material is it made?

14. What is common to the fictional Ered Luin mountains in Middle Earth, the Nilgiris in South India, and mountain chains in New South Wales, Congo, Jamaica and the Pacific Northwest?

14. FATHERS, SONS, GHOSTS

Our next trio is inspired by the Father, the Son and the Holy Ghost. Here we look at quiz questions inspired by famous fathers, equally famous sons, and of course popular beings from the other dimension who manifest before us as ghosts.

Set 1

1. Which founding father of his nation is known for his role in the Battle of Gallipoli during World War I, and for his successful war against Allied forces who aimed to partition his country amongst themselves?

2. Which son was told by his father at the age of ten, "My boy, you must find a kingdom big enough for your ambitions. My kingdom is too small for you," when the son tamed a horse that refused to be mounted by detecting its fear of its own shadow?

3. The Chudail, or churel, is a mythical demonic creature in Indian folklore. She resembles a woman and is described as hideous but able to shapeshift into a beautiful woman to lure men into the woods to kill them. What distinctive anatomical feature is a chudail considered to have, which helps identify them as such?

4. Which famous son made his acting debut in the critically acclaimed 2006 film *The Pursuit of Happyness*, winning an award for breakthrough performance at the MTV Music Awards?

5. Which 2003 Indian dystopian film depicts a future in an Indian village populated exclusively by men due to female infanticide over the years?

6. Which famous literary character appears three times in the story – the first to Horatio and a duo of soldiers named Bernardo and Marcellus, and the second and third to the lead character who shares his name?

7. The coronation of Bokassa I as the Emperor of Central Africa in 1976 cost over US$ 20 million and severe damage to the country's economy. The luxury and pomp were an exact replica of whose coronation in 1804?

8. Which politician, considered as the "Father of the Nation" in his country, was also popularly called *Bangabandhu* and served as head of state of the country from its independence until his assassination in a 1975 coup?

9. Naleba was an urban legend that went viral in the Indian state of Karnataka in the 1990s. The legend stated that a witch roamed the streets at night and knocked on the door. Those who opened their door would die. The residents took to writing Naleba on their doors. What did Naleba mean in Kannada, the local language?

10. And which 2018 Indian horror comedy film, starring Shraddha Kapoor, was loosely based on the Naleba urban legend?

11. Simon Bolivar, the military and political leader, was known as *El Libertador* or The Liberator for leading multiple countries in South America to independence from the Spanish Empire. Three of those modern-day countries are Venezuela, Colombia and Panama. Name the other three.

12. Which cricketer, a left-handed batsman and occasional slow left-arm orthodox bowler, represented Bengal in the Ranji Trophy? He played 11 international matches for India but was more famous for his 'other connection' to cricket.

13. What surname is shared by the illustrious father who played Dr. Erik Selvig in the Marvel Cinematic Universe, and the son who played Tarzan in the 2016 film *The Legend of Tarzan*?

14. Which Japanese manga series featured a teen genius who uses an otherworldly notebook belonging to a *shinigami* (grim reaper)? The notebook grants the user the supernatural ability to kill anyone whose name is written in its pages.

Set 2

1. Which Chinese physician and politician, known for his key role in the overthrow of the Qing dynasty during the 1911 Revolution, served as the provisional first President of the Republic of

China, and is referred to as the "Father of the Nation" in China?

2. Ghana follows a rigorous naming system for newborn children. The first name is a 'day name' based on the day of the week the child is born. The middle name refers to birth order, twin status, and ancestors. Common male names include Kwasi for boys born on a Sunday, Kojo on Monday, and Kwabena, Kaku, Kwaw and Kofi for the other days of the week. What common name is given to boys born on Saturday, also the first name of Ghana's first Prime Minister after independence?

3. How do we better know actor Jai Hemant _____, born on 2 March 1990, who made his debut in the Bollywood movie *Heropanti*? His actor father had his first big hit in a movie called *Hero*.

4. What character, created by Washington Irving, has been portrayed in film by Will Rogers, Jeff Goldblum, and Johnny Depp?

5. Which fictional ghost was beheaded with a blunt axe, leaving his head still attached to his neck by a thin strip of skin, preventing him from joining the Headless Hunt, a club for decapitated ghosts?

6. Which legendary ghost ship is said to never be able to make port, and is doomed to sail the oceans forever? The myth is said to have originated in the late 18th century and featured

prominently in the *Pirates of the Caribbean* movie franchise.

7. How do we know the nine kings of men who were given rings of power by the Dark Lord Sauron, and gained immortality but succumbed to his power, being reduced to invisible wraiths completely under Sauron's control?

8. Which 1988 Hollywood film features a recently deceased couple haunting their former home, and a devious poltergeist whose name sounds like a star and who can be summoned by calling his name three times?

9. Which first President of his country post-independence supported the Japanese occupation of his country in exchange for aid in spreading nationalist ideas, and then fought recolonization efforts before recognition of his country's independence in 1949?

10. Which TV show protagonist is the son of a retired police officer, and plays a radio host as well as a psychiatrist, the latter being a profession performed by his brother's character as well?

11. According to legend, his mother the Queen was poisoned while pregnant with him, but he was saved. The drop of poison had reached his forehead, which led to his name. Name this king, the son of a famous ruler who founded the dynasty as well as the father of a ruler who gave up war and promoted Buddhism across ancient Asia.

12. Which son, nicknamed *The Young Wolf*, takes over the rule of the North and rallies his forces after the execution of his father, and wins stunning victories until his death through betrayal in the third novel of the series?

13. Which ruler conquered the Median, Lydian and Neo-Babylonian empires, expanding his rule from the Mediterranean Sea to the Indus River? He is held in high regard among modern Iranians and is even mentioned in the Hebrew Bible.

14. Which politician is known in the country he founded as *Quaid-i-Azam* (Great Leader) and *Baba-i-Quam* (Father of the Nation)? He died just over a year after his country was formed.

Set 3

1. Which king of Magadha in ancient India died while being imprisoned by his son and successor, an event foreseen by the Buddha who had told the king that his son would be his enemy?

2. Which Academy Award-winning Disney-Pixar film tells the story of an overprotective clownfish who searches for his missing son in the company of a regal blue tang?

3. And which Disney film focuses on the love story of Kiara and Kovu, who also struggle to unite their estranged families and be together?

4. Who appeared as the ghost debunker Martin Heiss in the 2016 remake film *Ghostbusters* starring Melissa McCarthy?

5. Which political figure, known during his lifetime as *Bac* (Uncle), played a key role in the civil war and eventual unification of his country? The capital city of one of the country's halves was renamed in his honor in 1976.

6. Which son of Pepin the Short and King of the Franks has been called the "Father of Europe" because he united most of Western Europe for the first time since the Roman Empire? His most famous title was conferred on him by Pope Leo III in the year 800.

7. How do we better know Henry Junior, an archaeologist-cum-adventurer and the son of Henry Senior, a professor of medieval literature?

8. Which fictional protagonist, one of the most popular movie characters till date, grew up as a farmer on a desert planet before joining a rebel resistance and eventually confronting his evil father?

9. Which British royal family member was ranked number 49 on GQ's "50 Best Dressed Men in Britain" list in 2015?

10. Which fictional father figure was born with the last name Andolini in 1891, and escaped a local vendetta before emigrating to the USA as a boy? On his arrival in the USA, officials used his village name as his surname.

11. Marlon Brando famously portrayed the character in the above question. Which other fictional character did he portray in a superhero movie, charging $3.7 million and a share of the profits for less than 12 days of work and only 20 minutes of screen time?

12. The first of Oscar Wilde's stories to be published, which tale describes an American family who move to a castle haunted by the ghost of a dead English nobleman?

13. Which former Incan monarch was mummified, and later dug up by the Sanders-Hardiman expedition, with it being prophesied that all who desecrated his tomb would be rendered insane, while the mummy would call down a fireball to return back to where it came from? All part of the plot of a Tintin tale.

14. Which set of twenty-five moral stories is first recorded in the 11th century Sanskrit work *Kathasaritsagara*, and involves the discussions between a king and a reanimated corpse?

15. PLAYS, POEMS, PROSE

The trinity of literature. Stories as they are played out in front of audiences. Meanings within meanings outlined through poetry. Regular prose as well, as a matter of course.

Set 1

1. What plot device originated in Greek plays, with the goal of surprising the audience and resolving an otherwise irresolvable plot situation?

2. Which writer, known as *Upanyas Samrat* (Emperor among Novelists) by writers, began writing under the pen name "Nawab Rai" before switching to his more famous pen name?

3. Which old English epic poem by an unknown author is set in Scandinavia in the 6th century, and was made into a 2007 computer-animated film directed by Robert Zemeckis and starring the voices of Ray Winstone and Angelina Jolie?

4. Which 1818 novel, alternately titled *The Modern Prometheus*, tells the story of a young scientist who conducts an unorthodox scientific experiment? While the title refers to the name of the scientist, it has come to refer to his creation.

5. Which 1982 Bollywood film starring Sanjeev Kumar and Deven Vermain dual roles is based on Shakespeare's play *The Comedy of Errors*?

6. What 1847 novel, published under the pseudonym Ellis Bell, was the author's only finished novel and is set in a remote moorland farmhouse?

7. What epic poem, divided into 24 books, covers a duration of ten years in the life of its protagonist, and follows his journey home from a war he fought for ten years before the events of this book?

8. And which epic poem, published in 1667 and containing over ten thousand lines of verse, was written by its blind author entirely through dictation with the help of amanuenses and friends?

9. Which 1798 poem about the experiences of a sailor returning from a long sea voyage has been adapted into a 1975 film as well as a song by the heavy metal band Iron Maiden?

10. Which Sanskrit epic of 24,000 verses is considered the national epic of Cambodia, Thailand, Laos and Myanmar, in addition to being revered in India?

11. What term is used to describe theatrical performances presented in 41 professional theaters, each with 500 or more seats, located in the Theater District and Lincoln Center in midtown Manhattan in New York City?

12. In *Asterix and the Cauldron*, Asterix and Obelix try their hand at theater in order to make some money. The sequence includes Roman actors named Laurensolivius and Alecguinnus. What line does Obelix speak on stage which leads to the entire cast of the play being arrested?

13. Sophocles of Ancient Greece wrote over 120 plays of which only 7 have survived. Of these, his Theban plays, concerning the fate of Thebes during and after the reign of King Oedipus, include *Oedipus Rex*, *Oedipus at Colonus*, and which other third play?

14. The Belgian writer Noel Godin has written multiple books including one called *Cream and Punishment*. But what 1998 event in Brussels did he gain global attention for?

Set 2

1. Which 1959 novel by a Nobel Prize-winning writer, and which was adapted into a 1979 film that won the Academy Award for Best Foreign Language Film, revolves around the life of Oskar Matzerath, as narrated by himself?

2. Which novelist and supporter of Biafran independence from Nigeria was a titled Igbo chief and focused his novels on the clash of Western and traditional African values during and after the colonial era?

3. What sacred text, which according to theology contains writings of ancient prophets who lived

on the American continent from 2200 BC to 421 AD, is also the title of an Award-winning Broadway musical by Trey Parker and Matt Stone, the creators of South Park?

4. Which late 18th century English poet and painter was largely unrecognized during his own lifetime, but is now considered a seminal figure of the Romantic Age? His works figure prominently in the American crime TV show *The Mentalist*.

5. What form of verse, usually humorous and sometimes rude, follows a strict rhyme scheme, and appeared in England in the early 18th century before being popularized by Edward Lear in the 19th century?

6. Which Aldous Huxley novel was written in 1921 in the Tuscan seaside resort of Forte dei Marmi and describes a house party viewed through the eyes of Denis Stone?

7. Which popular Indian playback singer made his acting debut in the 2015 Marathi film *Katyar Kaljat Ghusali* (A dagger through the heart), based on the play of the same name?

8. Which fictional character first appeared in the adult novel *The Little White Bird* in 1902, and was described as a seven-day-old baby who flies from his nursery to Kensington Gardens in London? The character was made the center of his own play in 1904, and the play was then adapted into a novel in 1911 by the author.

9. Whose first play tells the story of the love of Agnimitra, the Shunga Emperor at Vidisha, for Malavika, the handmaiden of his chief queen?

10. Which Indian author and former investment banker, known for naming the protagonists in his novels after Lord Krishna, won a Filmfare Award for Best Screenplay for the film *Kai Po Che* which is based on one of his novels?

11. In the 2004 film Spider-Man 2, which Oscar Wilde play is Kirsten Dunst's character Mary Jane seen acting in?

12. Which Rudyard Kipling poem was written as a tribute to Leander Starr Jameson who attempted to overthrow the Boer government? The third and fourth lines of the second stanza of the poem are written on the wall of the players' entrance to the Center Court at Wimbledon.

13. The novel *The Grasshopper Lies Heavy*, which talks of an alternate universe where the Axis Powers lost World War II, is set within which alternate history novel written by Philip K Dick?

14. Which book of 135 four-line verses by Hindi poet Harivansh Rai Bachchan tries to explain the complexity of life through four instruments – wine, the server, the cup and the pub or bar?

Set 3

1. How do we better know the poet Ricardo Eliecer Neftali Reyes Basoalto, who won the Nobel Prize for Literature in 1971, and served briefly as honorary consul for his country in Rangoon, the then capital of the British colony of Burma?

2. Which novel, one of the longest in the English language, follows four families during an eighteen-month period, and centers on Mrs. Rupa Mehra's efforts to arrange the marriage of her younger daughter Lata?

3. Which acclaimed play was first performed on Broadway on December 3 1947, and introduced Jessica Tandy and Marlon Brando, both virtual unknowns at the time, to mainstream audiences?

4. Which English writer, widely considered as a pornographer during his lifetime for the explicit descriptions of sex and use of unprintable four-letter words in his books, with Penguin Books was prosecuted (in a case they won) for publishing his most famous work in 1928?

5. Which Tamil epic poem of 4,861 lines is the tale of the eponymous daughter of Kovalan and Madhavi, who follows in her mother's footsteps as a dancer and Buddhist nun?

6. What term, popularized by John Stuart Mill in 1868 while denouncing the government's Irish land policy, is commonly used to describe works such as *Brave New World* by Aldous Huxley and *Nineteen Eighty-Four* by George Orwell?

7. Vishal Bhardwaj famously adapted three Shakespearean works into Bollywood films – *Maqbool* (based on *Macbeth*), *Omkara* (*Othello*) and *Haider* (*Hamlet*). *Maqbool* is set in the Mumbai underworld while *Omkara* is set in the gang warfare of Uttar Pradesh. Where was *Haider* set?

8. Which prolific poet, writer and composer released his first poems at the age of sixteen under the pseudonym *Bhanusimha* (Sun Lion) has five museums dedicated to him in Bangladesh?

9. Which bestselling novelist spent a significant amount of his childhood solving anagrams and crossword puzzles, and participating in elaborate treasure hunts devised by his mathematician father? The environment inspired similar themes in his novels, including the relationship between one of the protagonists and her grandfather in his most famous (and controversial) novel.

10. Which Indian poet, portrayed on screen by Bharat Bhushan and Naseeruddin Shah, was given the title of Dabir-ul-Mulk by the then Mughal Emperor?

11. Which play, first presented in 1913, is based on an eponymous Greek mythological figure who fell in love with one of his sculptures, and was adapted into an Academy Award-winning musical starring Audrey Hepburn?

12. Which series of eight books and two short stories, spanning over 400 pages, was inspired by *The Lord of The Rings*, Arthurian legend, and *The Good, The*

Bad and The Ugly, and describes a gunslinger and his quest?

13. Which English poet and Poet Laureate of the United Kingdom is best remembered for *The Prelude*, a semi-autobiographical poem of his early years?

14. Which 1984 Bollywood film starring Shashi Kapoor, Rekha and Shekhar Suman is based on the Sanskrit play Mrichhakatika (The Clay Cart) by the ancient playwright Sudraka?

16. TRIOS, TRILOGIES, HAT TRICKS

In a quiz book about quiz trios, it was fitting that the last chapter should cover a trio of trios. This section looks at famous people who operated in trios, book and movie trilogies and sports hat tricks. I hope you have enjoyed the questions and thank you for reading so far.

Set 1

1. Chris Old famously took 4 wickets in 5 balls in a Test match for England vs Pakistan at Edgbaston in June 1978. He got Wasim Raja out with the second ball of his 19th over, Wasim Bari with the third, Iqbal Qasim with the fifth and Sikandar Bakht with the last ball of the over. What happened on the fourth ball of the over, which prevented his taking a hat-trick?

2. How do we collectively know Meteor Man, Vapor Man and Gravity Girl, who patrol space in their cruiser *Condor One* and maintain order while fighting evildoers in the name of the Galactic Patrol Law Enforcement Agency?

3. Which African American writer, the first to win the Hugo Award for Best Novel, went on to win it three years in a row for all three novels in her *Broken Earth* trilogy?

4. This trilogy started off as a sequel to the author's earlier 1937 work, and the original plot involved the protagonist running out of treasure and going on another adventure. But the author then expanded on a certain event from the 1937 work, and spent the next 12+ years writing over 9,000 pages of manuscripts. What trilogy, also adapted into an Academy Award-winning movie series?

5. Which celebrated trio make their last appearance in *The Man in the Iron Mask*, a sub-division of the novel *The Vicomte of Bragelonne: Ten Years Later*?

6. Which Pakistani cricketer, who shares his name with a Mughal Emperor, was the first to achieve a hat-trick in One Day International cricket, against Australia in 1982?

7. The 2010-11 Ashes series in Australia is known for the first England series win on Australian soil since 1986-87. But in one of the few bright spots for Australia in the series, which bowler took a hat-trick on the first day of the first test, thus also achieving the feat on his birthday?

8. Most gospels never mention their number, but they are believed to be three in number because of the number of gifts they carried. In some Eastern traditions they number twelve. There is also no explicit mention of their being kings, yet most traditions consider them so. Which trio am I talking about?

9. Which celebrated film trilogy had its music composed by the sitar maestro Ravi Shankar, and

describe the childhood, education and early adulthood of Apurba Kumar Roy?

10. Al Pacino is most well known for his role as Michael Corleone in the Godfather Trilogy, and received multiple nominations across the three movies. However, only one major award nominated him for the *Godfather Part III*. Which one?

11. What moniker is used to describe the anthropologist and paleontologist Louis Leakey's three protégés – Jane Goodall, Dian Fossey and Birute Galdikas – who he encouraged to work with chimpanzees, gorillas and orangutans respectively in their natural environments?

12. In which crime thriller TV series running from 1976-1981 did the TV actor John Forsythe give his voice for the unseen millionaire and titular character, who directs the activities of the main crime-fighting trio?

13. Which Australian cricketer is the only person to have taken two hat-tricks in the same Test match (at least as of January 2021)?

14. Which movie starred Tom Cruise as Austin Powers, Kevin Spacey as Dr. Evil, Danny DeVito as Mini-Me, and John Travolta as the titular villain?

Set 2

1. Chetan Sharma, Kapil Dev, Mohammad Shami and Kuldeep Yadav make up what illustrious list, with Kuldeep having his name on the list twice?

2. While the feat is known to have been performed before, HH Stephenson, playing for the All-England XI at Sheffield in 1858, was awarded something for achieving this feat. What did he do and what was he awarded?

3. In ancient Rome, the first triumvirate comprised Marcus Crassus, Pompey, and Julius Caesar. The second triumvirate included Marcus Lepidus and which other two statesmen?

4. Which acclaimed movie trilogy had 3 movies released 9 years apart, with each showing a few hours in the lives of the protagonists? The movies are set in Vienna, Paris and Greece.

5. While some of the other characters in the movies have called him Joe and Manco and Blondie, this character's name is never revealed throughout the trilogy of movies he plays the lead role in. Who portrayed this character with no name in one of the most iconic spaghetti western trilogies ever?

6. Which Dream works movie trilogy features creatures such as the Bewilderbeast, Changewing, Smothering Smokebreath, Flightmare and Night Fury, among others?

7. Which professional footballer, who also played country cricket, remains the only person to have scored a hat-trick in a football World Cup final?

8. What baseball term derives from hat-trick and is to describe a player striking out four times in a single game? A bigger hat is used since four is more than three.

9. Which crime-fighting trio was created when Professor Utonium added Chemical X to a mixture of "sugar, spice and everything nice"?

10. The Bollywood actress Ameeta Nangia is known for her roles in several movies, as well as TV shows such as *Hum Paanch* and *Tara*. Which animated trio of Disney characters did she voice dub for, in the Hindi version of the Disney show which Doordarshan viewers of the 1990s will be familiar with?

11. Who is the only footballer to have scored a hat-trick in two different football World Cups?

12. In the Japanese manga and anime franchise *Naruto*, ninja teams are set up in teams of 3 underlings (*genin*) led by a supervisor (*jonin*). What team number is Naruto's team, comprising himself, Sasuke Uchiha, Sakura Haruno and led by Hatake Kakashi?

13. Who were Harbhajan Singh's victims during his hat-trick in the second Test match for India against Australia, at Calcutta in 2001?

14. What region, described in Sumerian texts as a prominent trading partner of Sumer during the Middle Bronze Age, is most commonly associated with the Indus Valley civilization, and features prominently in a book trilogy by the Indian author Amish?

Set 3

1. Which acclaimed novel, the first of a trilogy, and known for popularizing the term 'cyberspace', popularized another term which became the name of a critically and publically acclaimed 1999 science fiction movie, also the first of a trilogy?

2. The 1945 Potsdam conference was held by the three Heads of state of the USSR, USA and UK to determine how to administer Germany after WWII. Who represented each country?

3. What contact sport, very popular in the Indian subcontinent, is known for having three variations called Sanjeevani, Gamini and Amar?

4. Which is till date the only FIFA football World Cup to feature no hat-tricks during the event?

5. Which legendary goal scorer, with 570 goals in 185 international matches, led India to a trio of Olympic gold medals from 1928 to 1936?

6. In the *Harold and Kumar* series of three movies, what fast-food chain do the protagonists Harold Lee and Kumar Patel try to go to after smoking marijuana?

7. What connects Maurice Allom of England, Peter Petherick of New Zealand, and Damien Fleming of Australia, for something they did in the years 1930, 1976 and 1994 respectively?

8. Who was the first Indian bowler to take a hat-trick in T20 internationals?

9. Which three dynasties made up the *Moovendhar*, or the Three Crowned Rulers, of the ancient Tamil country of Tamilakam in India?

10. What crime novel trilogy, originally planned as a ten-installment series by its author, was published posthumously after his 2005 death, and spawned a franchise which included a Hollywood film starring Daniel Craig?

11. What American sitcom, which aired from 1977 to 1984, focused on three single roommates Janet Wood, Chrissy Snow and Jack Tripper, who live together platonically in a California apartment complex?

12. The titular protagonist, Sloan Peterson and Cameron Frye skip school to spend a summer day in the city. Which movie is this, which the director described as his love letter to Chicago?

13. What trilogy of science fiction novels, published from 1938 to 1945, featured the philologist Elwin Ransom as a key protagonist?

14. Which 1983 film, the third of a trilogy, had its ending digitally altered after the release of a related 2004 film, also the third of a trilogy, to bolster the connection between the two sets of films?

ANSWERS

1. Love, Sex, Dhokha

  i.   Set 1

        i.   Romeo and Juliet

        ii. Sex, Lies and Videotape

        iii. Vidkun Quisling

        iv. Mandrake or Mandragora

        v.   Genghis Khan

        vi. Jagat Seth

        vii. "All you need is love" by the Beatles

        viii. Pan

        ix. Ephialtes

        x.   Kaikeyi

        xi. Rati

        xii. Eyes wide shut

        xiii. Hachiko the dog – waited at the station every day for his dead master to return

        xiv. Date rape drug

  ii. Set 2

        i.   Henry VIII of England

        ii. *Love in the Time of Cholera* by Gabriel Garcia Marquez

        iii. Patrice Lumumba

        iv. Ottoman Imperial Harem, or Ottoman Harem

        v.   Amsterdam

vi. Uranus
vii. RSAF (Royal Small Arms Factory)
viii. Warren Anderson
ix. Pocahontas
x. Sydney Carton in the Charles Dickens novel *A Tale of Two Cities*
xi. Lolita
xii. Vesper Lynd
xiii. Don Juan
xiv. March of the Penguins

iii. Set 3
   i. Guy Fawkes – for his involvement in the 1605 Gunpowder plot
   ii. Rodrigo Borgia
   iii. Eskimo kiss
   iv. The husbands of Elizabeth Taylor – she was married 8 times, including twice to Richard Burton
   v. Charles Ponzi, known for the Ponzi scheme
   vi. Mills and Boon
   vii. Steely Dan
   viii. *Love Story* by Erich Segal
   ix. Devadasi system
   x. Natwarlal
   xi. Kim Philby
   xii. Pheromones
   xiii. InsaafkaTarazu

xiv. Shashanka

2. Solid, Liquid, Gas
    i. Set 1
- i. Superconductivity
- ii. Molotov cocktail
- iii. Rainbow agents
- iv. Stained glass
- v. Dettol
- vi. Antoine Lavoisier, who among other things discovered the role of oxygen in combustion
- vii. Valyrian Steel
- viii. The Davy Lamp, named after his inventor Sir Humphry Davy
- ix. Dragon's blood
- x. Quicksilver
- xi. Betelgeuse
- xii. Mississippi mud pie
- xiii. Singapore Sling
- xiv. Neptune. Unlike the Great Red Spot, the Great Dark Spot is not one but a series of spots seen on Neptune's surface.

    ii. Set 2
- i. Conglomerate
- ii. Moraine
- iii. Dry cleaning
- iv. Neon signs
- v. Decompression sickness / The Bends

vi.   Hydrogen peroxide

vii.   Saccharin

viii.   Kryptonite, because it weakens Superman

ix.   Amrut

x.   Aether (also called ether)

xi.   Maximum particle diameter in micrometers / microns

xii.   Zamzam well

xiii.   Cavorite, from HG Wells' *The First Men in the Moon*

xiv.   Baku

iii.   Set 3

    i.   Alchemy

    ii.   Zepellins

    iii.   Ice palaces/houses

    iv.   Cork, used in wine bottle stoppers

    v.   Aerosol

    vi.   Will-o'-the-wisp

    vii.   Sarin gas

    viii.   Flubber

    ix.   Mohs scale of mineral hardness

    x.   Lagoon

    xi.   Emulsions

    xii.   Unobtainium

    xiii.   Chlorofluorocarbons (CFCs)

    xiv.   Laudanum

3. **Roti, Kapda, Makaan**
    i. Set 1
        i. Indian Prime Minister Narendra Modi – it had his full name embroidered on the fabric to resemble golden pinstripes
        ii. Mukesh Ambani's residence Antilia
        iii. Kulcha
        iv. Peach Melba, named after the Australian soprano Nellie Melba
        v. Birkin bags, named after the actress Jane Birkin
        vi. The White House
        vii. South Court, also known as Jinnah House
        viii. Chicken soup
        ix. Vietnam
        x. Specifications for making the National flag of India
        xi. Kohinoor diamond
        xii. Priest holes, to hide Catholic priests
        xiii. Salsa
        xiv. Airbnb

    ii. Set 2
        i. Nori seaweed, used in sushi
        ii. Savile Row
        iii. Asgard

iv. Queen Elizabeth ascended to the throne while staying there

v. The 2009 movie *Up*. He uses helium balloons to carry his house.

vi. Nylon

vii. Paella

viii. Tweed

ix. Kati roll

x. Spaghetti sauce (Accept: marinara)

xi. Chorizo

xii. Shahtoosh shawl

xiii. DakshinGangotri

xiv. Buckingham Palace & Windsor Castle

iii. Set 3

i. Po'boy – from poor boy

ii. Jodhpur. Hence, it is called a Jodhpuri

iii. Chikan

iv. Café du Monde

v. Adobe

vi. Yurt

vii. Gandhi cap, named after Mahatma Gandhi. The resurgence was in the wake of the Anna Hazare anti-corruption movement.

viii. Crepes

ix. Scotch eggs

  x. Corset

  xi. Snow. Air pockets trapped in snow make it a good insulator.

  xii. Oysters Rockefeller, named after John D. Rockefeller, the then wealthiest American, for the richness of the dish.

  xiii. Ascot racecourse

  xiv. Xanadu

4. Germany, Italy, Japan

  i. Set 1

   i. The flag of Bavaria has blue and white colors

   ii. Augustus

   iii. Hattori Hanzo

   iv. Oskar Schindler, of *Schindler's List* fame

   v. Cicero, the ancient Roman orator

   vi. Edo period. Edo is the former name of Tokyo.

   vii. Colosseum of Rome

   viii. Rudolph Hess flew to Scotland, seemingly to seek his help broking a peace treaty between Britain and Germany

   ix. The 42-line Bible

   x. Port Arthur

   xi. Regnal eras in Japan. The Heisei era ended with the abdication of Emperor Akihito on 30 Apr

2019, and the Reiwaera of Emperor Naruhito started the next day.

    xii. Libya

   xiii. Vercingetorix

   xiv. Amaterasu

ii.   Set 2

      i. Speyer

     ii. Victor Emmanuel III

    iii. Redshirts. Giuseppe Garibaldi was in exile in Uruguay at the time.

    iv. Namibia, formerly South West Africa

     v. Dachau concentration camp

    vi. Tanuki, or Japanese raccoon dog

   vii. Tatami mats

  viii. BASF

    ix. Padua

     x. Manga

    xi. Florence

    xii. Wilhelm Roentgen, for his discovery of X-rays

   xiii. *Godzilla*. It is the longest continuously running movie franchise.

   xiv. Marcel Grossmann

iii.   Set 3

      i. Switzerland, and the Papal Swiss Guard

ii. Toshiro Mifune

iii. Letters from Iwo Jima & Flags of Our Fathers

iv. Two Women (*La ciociara*)

v. Oktoberfest

vi. Immanuel Kant

vii. Vienna sausage (Wiener Würstchen)

viii. Rei Shimura

ix. Sardinia

x. Dragon Ball

xi. Salvator Mundi

xii. Okinawa

xiii. West Germany, in the 1954 FIFA World Cup final

xiv. These Romans are crazy. Immortalized in the Asterix comics.

5. **Army, Navy, Air Force**
   i. Set 1
      i. PNS Ghazi – the Pakistan Navy submarine which was sunk during the 1971 India-Pakistan War
      ii. Sudas
      iii. First use of an airplane in warfare
      iv. Akshauhini
      v. Vijaydurg
      vi. Bockscar, or Bock's Car
      vii. Sir Douglas Bader

viii. Entebbe, Uganda – the Israel forces successfully carried out a hostage rescue mission
  ix. Afzal Khan
   x. Srivijaya, in present-day Indonesia
  xi. Agincourt
 xii. INS Vikrant
xiii. Bajaj 'V'
 xiv. Guernica, Spain

ii. Set 2
   i. The Terracotta Army of China
  ii. The Hunt for Red October. Red October is a submarine.
 iii. Napalm
 iv. Ephialtes
   v. Salamis
 vi. Manfred von Richthofen, the Red Baron
vii. Cravat, from Croat
viii. Bashi-Bazouk
  ix. Battle of Red Cliffs. The John Woo film was called *Red Cliff*.
   x. Operation Grandslam
  xi. Iron Cross
 xii. Lusitania
xiii. Marut (the full name is HAL HF-24 Marut)
 xiv. Operation Pawan

iii. Set 3
  i. The 1982 Falklands War between Argentina and the United Kingdom, for the Falkland Islands
  ii. Trishna
  iii. Kamikaze. The country is Japan.
  iv. Lieutenant
  v. Territorial Army
  vi. Francis Drake
  vii. Vijeta
  viii. Lakshya
  ix. Anwar Sadat of Egypt
  x. Natal
  xi. Top Gun
  xii. Hot Shots
  xiii. Fort William in Kolkata, India
  xiv. Charles Darwin. The ship is the HMS Beagle.

6. Agriculture, Industry, Services
i. Set 1
  i. Mehrgarh
  ii. Kanchipuram, known for its silk saris.
  iii. Uberization, after Uber
  iv. Actuary
  v. Guild
  vi. Svalbard Global Seed Vault
  vii. New World crops

viii. The Ford Model T car was released only in the black color
ix. Obamacare
x. Reuters
xi. The Kalka-Shimla railway, allowing the British colonial government to move from Calcutta, the winter capital, to Shimla, the summer capital
xii. Green Revolution
xiii. India
xiv. DDT

ii. Set 2
  i. Stanford University
  ii. IIT Kharagpur
  iii. IKEA. The name is an acronym of his initials, along with the initials of his farm and village.
  iv. Nitrogen fixation
  v. El Nino
  vi. MacAdam method of road construction
  vii. Old Man Trump, about Fred Trump
  viii. Aravind Eye Hospitals
  ix. Jethro Tull
  x. Apple Inc.
  xi. The Road to Wigan Pier
  xii. Starwood Preferred Guest
  xiii. Babe

xiv. The Dutch East India Company (in Dutch, the *Vereenigde Oostindische Compagnie*)

iii. Set 3

    i. The annual flooding of the Nile

    ii. Andrew Thomas (AT) Kearney

    iii. LIC – Life Insurance Corporation of India

    iv. Gregor Mendel, considered the father of the science of genetics

    v. Antwerp, Belgium

    vi. Grafting

    vii. Indigo dye

    viii. NR Narayana Murthy who founded Infosys

    ix. Time Warner Cable

    x. Portland cement

    xi. Potatoes

    xii. Maize

    xiii. DuPont

    xiv. The two variants of smallpox, which was finally certified as eradicated in 1980

7. Past, Present, Future

i. Set 1

    i. The Code of Hammurabi, the code of law in ancient Mesopotamia

    ii. None other than Savarkar himself

    iii. Crack of Doom

iv. Leicester City winning the English Premier League in 2015-16

v. All four statues show Pharaoh Rameses II

vi. Nostradamus

vii. Tachyons

viii. The 2015 World Cup

ix. Francisco Pizarro

x. Mason-Dixon line, known informally as the border between the Northern and Southern states

xi. Pre-1989 graffiti was only on the Western side of the wall, as the eastern side was zealously guarded by East German soldiers

xii. A Christmas Carol, by Charles Dickens

xiii. All are named in honor of European monarchs

xiv. Miroslav Klose

ii. Set 2

i. Futurism

ii. Robert Hooke, who discovered Hooke's Law

iii. Malaria

iv. The Jetsons

v. Sybil Trelawney, from the world of Harry Potter

vi. Bachpan Bachao Andolan

vii. Rose line, used to refer to the Paris Meridian in the Dan Brown novel 'The Dan Vinci Code'

viii. Krakatoa, known for the explosive volcanic eruption in 1883

ix. Multiple winners of the Booker Prize for Fiction

x. Morlocks, from HG Wells' *The Time Machine*

xi. Interstellar

xii. Emperor Hirohito of Japan. The statement was made following Japan's surrender in World War II

xiii. Gangaikonda Cholapuram

xiv. The Vietnam War

iii. Set 3

i. Kadamba Transport Corporation of Goa, named after the Kadamba dynasty

ii. The Red Fort in Delhi

iii. They all lie on the mid-Atlantic Ridge

iv. 21 December 2012

v. Ray Kurzweil

vi. Timecop

vii. Inside the Saudi Arabian consulate

viii. Daulatabad

ix. Ibn Battuta

x. Hans Rosling
xi. Back to the Future. The car, of course, is the DMC DeLorean.
xii. Winston Churchill
xiii. *Go Set a Watchman*, by Harper Lee
xiv. Accenture, from 'Accent on the Future'

8. USA, USSR, NAM
i. Set 1

    i. Cuban Missile Crisis
    ii. Vostok
    iii. Belgrade
    iv. Josip Broz 'Tito'
    v. Iron Curtain
    vi. Watergate
    vii. Vietnam War
    viii. Perestroika and glasnost, popularized by Mikhail Gorbachev during the final years of the USSR
    ix. Neelam Sanjiva Reddy, former President of India
    x. United Nations Secretary-General Dag Hammerskjold
    xi. Vasily Zaitsev
    xii. Gary Powers
    xiii. Bikini Atoll, the site of US nuclear tests from 1946 to 1958
    xiv. The Russian exclave of Kaliningrad, formerly known as

Konigsberg. The math problem was *The Seven Bridges of Konigsberg*.

ii. Set 2

    i. Cyprus and Malta. They ended their NAM membership when they joined the Eurozone in 2004.

    ii. Space Force

    iii. Lech Walesa, the former President of Poland

    iv. Operation Condor

    v. Gamal Abdel Nasser, the then President of Egypt

    vi. Aral Sea

    vii. Bosnian War from 1992-95

    viii. The Baltic States – Latvia, Lithuania and Estonia

    ix. Taiwan

    x. Cuba

    xi. North and South Korea

    xii. Bonn, the former capital of West Germany

    xiii. 1976

    xiv. Their refusal to participate under the presidency of Venezuela, as their governments did not recognize Nicolas Maduro's government

   iii.   Set 3
  - i. MN Roy
  - ii. Tintin, in *Tintin in the Land of the Soviets*
  - iii. From Russia with Love
  - iv. Checkpoint Charlie in Berlin
  - v. Idi Amin of Uganda
  - vi. *Communist Manifesto* by Karl Marx and Friedrich Engels
  - vii. Indonesia
  - viii. Ghana
  - ix. Laos, during the Laotian Civil War and Vietnam War
  - x. Norodom Sihanouk
  - xi. The United States admitted the former Shah for cancer treatment
  - xii. Kuwait
  - xiii. Romania
  - xiv. Angola

9. DC, Marvel, Everyone else

   i.   Set 1
  - i. Watchmen
  - ii. Pavitr Prabhakar, the Indian version of Spiderman who debuted in Spiderman: India
  - iii. Riverdale from the Archie Comics universe
  - iv. Calisota, from California and Minnesota

v. George Clooney. All actors who portrayed Batman in films.

vi. Doctor Octopus from Spiderman

vii. The Spear of Destiny

viii. Thor. Thursday is named after Thor.

ix. The Human Torch, in the *Fantastic Four* films

x. Best Sound Editing

xi. Salem, from the *Sabrina the Teenage Witch* series

xii. Sign up for and star in the *Green Lantern* movie

xiii. Richie Rich

xiv. Dogs and frogs, respectively

ii. Set 2

i. They have all portrayed Catwoman in films

ii. *Guardians of the Galaxy*

iii. *Daredevil*

iv. *300*

v. Sin City

vi. They dream about actors playing themselves in the real world. The Martian Manhunter doesn't have this dream because he doesn't feature in any media at the time.

vii. Thanos. Thanos is short for Athanasios which means immortal.

viii. Sandman

ix.   Mark Hamill

x.   Wakanda, home of the Black Panther

xi.   The Paris Peace Accords

xii.   The League of Extraordinary Gentlemen

xiii.   Nanotechnology

xiv.   Neurosurgeon

iii.   Set 3

i.   Atlantis, the home of Aquaman

ii.   All are alter-egos of Calvin, from the comic strip *Calvin and Hobbes*

iii.   Spiderman, in *Spiderman: Into the Spider-Verse*

iv.   Road to Perdition

v.   Snowy the Dog from *The Adventures of Tintin*. The original French version was Milou.

vi.   Idefix, a pun on idee fixe. The English version is Dogmatix.

vii.   V for Vendetta

viii.   Teen Titans

ix.   Marlon Brando

x.   Alkali Lake in the X-Men series

xi.   Captain Marvel. He is now known as Shazam.

xii.   Bifrost

xiii.   Spawn

xiv.   Kingsman: The Secret Service

10. British, French, Portuguese rules

i. Set 1

    i. The Black Hole of Calcutta

    ii. Francois Bernier

    iii. Carnation Revolution, which overthrew the authoritarian Estado Novo regime

    iv. Robert Clive

    v. Chandannagar

    vi. Timoji/Timmayya

    vii. The British, who were allied with the Portuguese during the Napoleonic Wars

    viii. The Maratha king Shivaji

    ix. Buxar

    x. The Treaty of Amritsar

    xi. Cardinal Richelieu

    xii. Dadra and Nagar Haveli

    xiii. Baroda, Mysore, Gwalior, Jammu & Kashmir and Hyderabad

    xiv. Fort St. David

ii. Set 2

    i. Goa. It was introduced in 1869 when Goa was elevated from the status of a Portuguese colony to an overseas possession.

    ii. Bartle Frere was the administrator of Sindh province. The stamp was named after the then British name for Sindh, and the British word for Daak, the Hindi word for post.

   iii. Karaikal, in 1739

   iv. Dr. Ram Manohar Lohia

   v. Ryotwari system

   vi. Denmark. The town was originally called Tranquebar.

   vii. *Saat Hindustani* (Seven Indians)

   viii. Tristao de Braganza Cunha

   ix. Port Blair, the capital of Andaman and Nicobar Islands, is named after him

   x. The Kohinoor diamond

   xi. Pulicat

   xii. £10 per annum

   xiii. RSAF (Royal Small Arms Factory) Enfield

   xiv. Spain

iii. Set 3

   i. Kochi/Cochin

   ii. Allahabad

   iii. Tipu Sultan

   iv. Lusufonia Games

   v. 1877. Queen Victoria had been Queen for 40 years, when she added *Empress of India* to her list of titles.

   vi. Xendiis a local term for the top knot hair style of Hindus

   vii. Denmark

   viii. Madras (now called Chennai)

ix. St. Francis Xavier

x. Our Lady of the Immaculate Conception Church

xi. Andaman and Nicobar Islands

xii. Pakistan

xiii. Burma/Myanmar

xiv. Lord Irwin, later known as Earl Halifax

11. Brain, Brawn, Beauty

i. Set 1

i. Reykjavik, Iceland

ii. Norway

iii. Light was considered 'divine' – more light had to be let into the churches

iv. The World Trade Center in New York

v. Pakistan

vi. Indians to win the Miss World title

vii. Chanakya (also known as Kautilya)

viii. Arnold Schwarzenegger. The event is the Arnold Sports Festival.

ix. Gal Gadot

x. Srinivasa Ramanujam

xi. Tom Moody

xii. The skin-lightening product *Fair and Lovely* was renamed *Glow and Lovely*

142

xiii. Barbie

xiv. Sabu, from the *Chacha Chaudhary* series by Diamond Comics

ii. Set 2

    i. Glock handguns

    ii. Ugly Betty

    iii. Voltaire, born as Francois-Marie Arouet

    iv. The Great Gama

    v. Satyajit Ray

    vi. Nina Davuluri

    vii. Miss Black America

    viii. Galileo Galilei

    ix. Avicenna/Ibn Sina

    x. JuditPolgar

    xi. Dara Singh

    xii. Mallakhamba

    xiii. Jallikattu

    xiv. Bikini

iii. Set 3

    i. Amitabh Bachchan

    ii. Bob Dylan

    iii. Nikola Tesla. The SI unit of magnetic flux density was named in his honor.

    iv. Galileo Galilei and Isaac Newton

    v. Goliath

    vi. Blaise Pascal. The representation is Pascal's triangle.

    vii. Mark Spitz

ii. Tenochtitlan (now Mexico City)
iii. The Big Bang
iv. Gir Sanctuary, and the Asiatic Lion
v. Mughal-e-Azam
vi. Robert Oppenheimer, after the first detonation of a nuclear weapon
vii. Mitosis
viii. Gilgamesh
ix. Yosemite
x. Mozart's Last Requiem
xi. Pandora
xii. Salim Ali
xiii. Deep Impact
xiv. Mummification

iii. Set 3
i. Vermont (formerly a part of New York)
ii. Athens, Greece
iii. 1972
iv. End of Days
v. Zombie. The 1968 movie was *Night of the Living Dead*.
vi. The Indian state of Kerala
vii. Bishnois
viii. Nemesis
ix. Romulus and Remus, who are believed to have founded the city of Rome
x. Chipko movement

xi. Bamian Buddhas in Afghanistan

xii. Kosovo

xiii. Cheetah

xiv. Skynet, from the *Terminator* movie franchise

13. Red, Green, Blue

i. Set 1

    i. Cardinal

    ii. Libya

    iii. Azure

    iv. The Chicago river

    v. Maroon. The band is Maroon 5.

    vi. Lapis Lazuli

    vii. Sultan Ahmed Mosque in Istanbul

    viii. The Statue of Liberty

    ix. Traffic lights

    x. *The Starry Night* by Vincent van Gogh

    xi. Leprechaun

    xii. Burgundy

    xiii. Seeing red

    xiv. Iron oxide

ii. Set 2

    i. Red giant

    ii. Picasso's Blue Period

    iii. BB King

    iv. Absinthe

    v. The Emerald City (from *The Wizard of Oz*)

vi. Blue chip stock

vii. Greece

viii. Billiards (Snooker/Pool will do too)

ix. Leaf color in autumn/fall

x. Red herring

xi. Methane

xii. Levi's, the main product being jeans

xiii. Jojo Rabbit

xiv. The Missionaries of Charity

iii. Set 3

i. Chromium

ii. Fiddler's green

iii. Santa Claus

iv. Neelkanth (literally, blue throat)

v. South Korea. The house is formally called *Cheongwadae* or "pavilion of blue tiles"

vi. Tuaregs

vii. Austria

viii. Guacamole

ix. The Mentalist

x. Robb Stark

xi. Hematite – iron oxide

xii. Green tea

xiii. Jade

xiv. All of them are known as the 'Blue Mountains'

14. Fathers, Sons, Ghosts

i. Set 1

    i. Mustafa Kemal Ataturk, the founding father of modern Turkey

    ii. Alexander the Great

    iii. A chudail's feet are turned backwards

    iv. Jaden Smith

    v. Matrubhoomi

    vi. The Ghost of Hamlet's Father, from the play *Hamlet*

    vii. Napoleon Bonaparte, who was crowned Emperor of the French

    viii. Sheikh Mujibur Rahman

    ix. Come tomorrow

    x. *Stree*

    xi. Bolivia, Ecuador and Peru

    xii. Rohan Gavaskar, the son of Sunil Gavaskar

    xiii. Skarsgard

    xiv. Death Note

ii. Set 2

    i. Sun Yat-Sen

    ii. Kwame (Nkrumah)

    iii. Tiger Shroff, son of Jackie Shroff

    iv. Ichabod Crane, from *The Legend of Sleepy Hollow*

    v. Sir Nicholas de Mimsy-Porpington, also known as Nearly

       Headless Nick (from the Harry Potter universe)
vi. The *Flying Dutchman*
vii. Nazgul or Ringwraiths
viii. Beetlejuice
ix. Sukarno of Indonesia
x. Frasier Crane
xi. Bindusara, the son of Chandragupta Maurya and the father of Emperor Ashoka
xii. Robb Stark, from the *A Song of Ice and Fire* series
xiii. Cyrus the Great, founder of the first Persian Empire
xiv. Muhammad Ali Jinnah

iii. Set 3
    i. Bimbisara
    ii. *Finding Nemo*
    iii. *The Lion King II: Simba's Pride*
    iv. Bill Murray, the lead character from the original *Ghostbusters* film
    v. Ho Chi Minh
    vi. Charlemagne. He was crowned 'Emperor of the Romans' in 800.
    vii. Indiana Jones
    viii. Luke Skywalker
    ix. Prince George of Cambridge, at the age of one
    x. Vito Corleone
    xi. Jor-El
    xii. The Canterville Ghost

xiii. Rascar Capac

xiv. Vikram and Betal

15. Plays, Poems, Prose

   i. Set 1

      i. Deus ex machina (literally 'God from the machine')

      ii. Premchand (born as Dhanpat Rai Srivastava)

      iii. Beowulf

      iv. Frankenstein

      v. Angoor

      vi. *Wuthering Heights*

      vii. *The Odyssey* by Homer

      viii. *Paradise Lost* by John Milton

      ix. "Rime of the Ancient Mariner"

      x. *Ramayana*

      xi. Broadway

      xii. Obelix's classic line "These Romans Are Crazy"

      xiii. Antigone

      xiv. He threw a pie in Bill Gates' face

   ii. Set 2

      i. *The Tin Drum* by Gunter Grass

      ii. Chinua Achebe

      iii. Book of Mormon

      iv. William Blake

      v. Limerick

      vi. Crome Yellow

      vii. Shankar Mahadevan

      viii. *Peter Pan* by JM Barrie

ix. Kalidasa

x. Chetan Bhagat

xi. The Importance of Being Earnest

xii. If–

xiii. *The Man in the High Castle*, wherein the Axis Powers have won WW2

xiv. Madhushala

Set 3

i. Pablo Neruda

ii. *A Suitable Boy* by Vikram Seth

iii. "A Streetcar Named Desire" by Tennessee Williams

iv. DH Lawrence. The book was *Lady Chatterley's Lover.*

v. Manimekalai

vi. Dystopia

vii. The Kashmir insurgency

viii. Rabindranath Tagore

ix. Dan Brown. The novel is *The Da Vinci Code.*

x. Ghalib

xi. "Pygmalion" by George Bernard Shaw

xii. *The Dark Tower* series by Stephen King

xiii. William Wordsworth

xiv. Utsav

16. Trios, Trilogies, Hat tricks

i. Set 1

    i. He bowled a no-ball!

    ii. Galaxy Trio

    iii. NK Jemisin

    iv. *The Lord of the Rings* by JRR Tolkien

    v. The Three Musketeers – Athos, Porthos and Aramis

    vi. Jalal-ud-din

    vii. Peter Siddle

    viii. The Three Magi

    ix. *The Apu Trilogy* by Satyajit Ray

    x. The Golden Globes

    xi. The Trimates. Also called Leakey's Angels.

    xii. Charlie's Angels

    xiii. Jimmy Mathews

    xiv. Austinpussy (the movie within the movie *Austin Powers in Goldmember*)

ii. Set 2

    i. Indian bowlers to take hat tricks in One Day Internationals

    ii. He took 3 wickets in 3 balls and was awarded a hat. Hence the term hat-trick!

    iii. Augustus Caesar (Octavian) and Mark Antony

    iv. The *Before* trilogy directed by Richard Linklater

v. Clint Eastwood. The trilogy in question is Sergio Leone's *Dollars* trilogy – *A Fistful of Dollars*, *For a Few Dollars More* and *The Good, The Bad and The Ugly*.

vi. *How to Train Your Dragon*

vii. Geoff Hurst

viii. Golden sombrero

ix. The Powerpuff Girls

x. Huey, Dewey, Louie in Duck Tales

xi. Gabriel Batistuta of Argentina. He achieved the feat in 1994 and 1998.

xii. Team 7

xiii. Ricky Ponting, Adam Gilchrist and Shane Warne

xiv. Meluha

iii. Set 3

i. *Neuromancer* by William Gibson. The term is 'Matrix'.

ii. Joseph Stalin from the USSR, Harry Truman from the USA, and Winston Churchill from the UK. Churchill was replaced midway by Clement Attlee after the latter won the 1945 elections in the UK.

iii. Kabaddi

iv. The 2006 World Cup in Germany

154

ABOUT THE AUTHOR

Sanat Pai Raikar is a husband and father, an analytics consultant by day and an avid quizzer and professional quizmaster the rest of the time. He has written the definitive article on 'quiz' for the Encyclopaedia Britannica.

Sanat's quizzing journey began with school quizzes where he was very active in the inter-school quiz contests in Goa where he grew up. He carried this fervor to college, where he led the NIT Trichy quiz team to the quarter-finals of BBC World's University Challenge in 2004. He led the English Literary and Quiz Society of NIT Trichy, "Balls by Picasso" as well as "Atharva", the quiz club at IIM Kozhikode where he continued his studies.

A hectic work schedule across startups and continents hasn't dampened Sanat's enthusiasm for quizzing over the years. He co-founded Quizarre with his wife Nirupama. Quizarre provides quiz, crossword and puzzle content to entrance exam content aggregators and publications.

Always on the lookout for good questions (as well as good answers to the questions), Sanat describes himself as a lifelong learner whose aim is to make quizzing fun for everyone.

Lightning Source UK Ltd.
Milton Keynes UK
UKHW010633151221
395665UK00004B/200